INTRODUCING SOCIAL CHANGE

A MANUAL FOR

AMERICANS

OVERSEAS

INTRODUCING SOCIAL CHANGE

by CONRAD M. ARENSBERG

Professor of Anthropology, Columbia University

and ARTHUR H. NIEHOFF

Research Scientist, Human Resources Research Office,
The George Washington University

ALDINE PUBLISHING COMPANY / *Chicago*

First published 1964 by
ALDINE Publishing Company
320 West Adams Street
Chicago, Illinois 60606

Library of Congress Catalog Card Number 64-25356

Designed by David Miller

Printed in the United States of America

Second printing 1965
Third printing 1966

CONTENTS

INTRODUCING SOCIAL CHANGE

1

INTRODUCTION

☐ **THE CHALLENGE**

The United States is now in the forefront of a great effort to spread new objects, ideas, techniques and financial assistance to the presently less favored nations of the world. From the point of view of technological and financial ability, no nation has ever been in a more favorable position to lead such an effort.

There are many types of Americans, as well as other Westerners, who are involved in this work. There are government technical advisors directly concerned with improving the economic circumstances of people in these other lands. There are members of philanthropic foundations and private citizens engaged in the same work. There are businessmen, who, though they may primarily be concerned with profit for their own companies, are still involved in assisting the nations where they operate because business thrives only where people can afford to buy the products. There are missionaries, who at one time may have been interested only in disseminating their faith but are now concerned with assisting the people of countries where they work.

New ideas have always passed from people to people, from nation to nation, until some of them have blanketed the earth. We know that some of the plants domesticated by the American Indians, such as corn, tobacco and potatoes, travelled around the world within three hundred years. The use of

1

firearms was adopted by non-Western people practically everywhere these devices became available. In the realm of new ideas we know that democracy, even though it has usually been modified, has travelled to many of the countries of Asia, Africa, and Latin America.

Ideas of the supernatural have also travelled far from the countries where they originated. We know that Buddhism arose in North India but spread to all the countries of South and East Asia before it went into decline in its homeland. From the Middle East came Christianity, Islam and Judaism, belief systems that were carried to all parts of the world, to hundreds of millions of people of all races. If there is any generalization about the nature of man that is absolutely true, it is that he borrows new things, ideas, and techniques from his neighbor, whether this neighbor is of his own kind or from another culture.

There are some differences, however, between the transfer of ideas in former times and the transfers in the present century. Much, if not most, of the transfer of ideas in earlier centuries was not done deliberately, at least on the part of the donor peoples.

For instance, the American Indians, as far as we know, had no particular desire to spread the seeds and techniques for growing corn and tobacco to other peoples, not to mention the methods of consuming these products. It was the explorers who picked up the ideas when they saw the Indians smoking tobacco or eating corn, and who carried the seeds and knowledge for growing the plants and consuming them back to Europe, and from there on to Asia and Africa. It was thus with firearms also, even though the transfer of the thing and the technique was in the other direction. The Indians saw the power of a gun when some of them were killed through its use. They then tried in every way they could to get this new device. It has been like this even with ideas.

Most of the nations of Africa and Asia that now claim to be democracies picked up the idea on their own, often in situations of conflict with the European powers that were dominating them. Indeed, many Asian and African leaders have spent many years of their lives in prisons because they supported the idea of democracy and self-government for their own countries. The one set of ideas which Westerners deliberately tried to give others in earlier times was religion. The Christian missionary has tried to transfer his idea of the supernatural to people of other cultures since the beginning of the Christian era. But with the exception of the missionary effort, there has been no large-scale organized effort on the part of Westerners to give to other nations their ideas.

We have deliberately used the verb "to give" because there have been deliberate efforts by the United States and other Western nations to influence other countries earlier than the twentieth century. But these have not normally been "given." European colonial powers and the United States imposed changes on the dependencies that were under their domination for a variety of reasons, varying all the way from genuine desires to assist them in their development to out-and-out economic exploitation. Regardless of the motives, the changes were not voluntarily accepted by the recipient countries.

In contrast, the spread of new ideas and techniques from the West that has gone on since World War II has been on a cooperative basis. No American or any other Westerner, whether a government official, a private businessman, or a missionary, can enforce his presence or impose his ideas on the people he is working with if they don't want him there. National sovereignty is the rule now, which means that *change must be accepted voluntarily by the host people.*

A final difference is that change in previous centuries, because it was not a deliberate effort by the donors, often took long periods of time, even hundreds and thousands of years. It took three to four thousand years for new food-growing techniques to spread from the Middle East to Europe. Nowadays, almost all change is expected to take place rapidly, both by the donors and the recipients. Both we and they think in terms of years or at most of decades. In contrast to the 3,000-year movement of food-growing ideas from the Middle East to Europe, the less developed countries of the world expect new food-growing and processing techniques to become effec-

tive within their "five-year plans." We are living in what has
been termed "the decade of development." ✓

It might appear that a superior technique of growing crops,
healing the sick, educating the young, or processing wool
would automatically be accepted by those lacking such techniques. If the time required were of no significance, or if the
new techniques were imposed by law, they would probably
be accepted in due course. On the other hand, if the changes
are to take place voluntarily and in a relatively short time, the
problem is considerably greater than merely explaining or
demonstrating the new ideas to the recipient people. We, the
transmitters of these new ideas, have a specific body of customs and beliefs which differ in many respects from those of
the underdeveloped nations.

Such customs and beliefs constitute the culture of each
group of people and *understanding this culture can spell
the difference between success and failure in introducing new
ideas or methods*. Any professional person who has spent even
a minimum of time in some underdeveloped country can
relate instances when superior ideas or techniques failed to
be accepted by the local people only because their habits
and customs were not understood by the innovators. The two
following instances will illustrate this kind of problem.

A few years ago in Laos an American drilling company
drove a number of good, deep wells for the benefit of villagers.
The villagers were well aware of the advantages of having a
constant source of good water and were quite happy to abandon the water holes and intermittent streams which they had
formerly used. However, within two years almost three-quar-
ters of the wells were out of commission. The villagers were
unhappy about the situation but did not know how to repair
the pumps. Although the job was not very difficult, some source
of advice and parts was needed to keep them operative. The
well drillers had ignored the problem of maintenance and the
low level of technical competence of the villagers. Nor had the
drillers attempted to ascertain which villagers were best suited
to be responsible for the wells. They had worked with the

headman of each village, but this person had only limited authority and assumed little responsibility for the wells.

By chance, wells had been drilled in Buddhist temple grounds in a couple of villages. These had been maintained, had been repaired when broken, and even the area around them had been kept clean and orderly. The Buddhist monks probably had far more respect and ability to organize the villagers than did the secular headmen. If all the wells had been put in temple grounds, there might have been a far smaller maintenance problem. A respectful attitude toward Buddhist monks and a willingness to cooperate with them is part of the culture of most Southeast Asian countries; a knowledge of this, tied to a technical improvement (a driven well), could have spelled success. In this instance, the technical improvement alone proved a failure.

Another example of failure due to lack of understanding of the cultural values and beliefs of a people, in this case ideas of ritual purity, comes from India. This time American change agents attempted to introduce a system of sanitary latrines into a rural village complex. To the Americans, latrines constituted a decided improvement for the health conditions of the local population. However, the basic concepts of public health on which the Americans based their project decision were not shared by the Indian villagers. The villagers did not know that germs were carried by the flies which had lived in the fecal material. Furthermore, the latrines as devised by the American innovators were inconvenient. The women had to carry extra water for flushing them and the men had to return from the fields to use them. The women also objected to latrines because in the old system they went on little expeditions for elimination each day, to areas where other women came. These trips were enjoyed by women because they could relax and gossip as well as take care of their bodily functions.

Probably most important, however, was the fact that these Indian villagers regarded human excrement and anything in contact with it as very defiling. They thus regarded the latrines as focuses of defilement and were reluctant to have them near their houses. The innovators had, of course, introduced the latrines on the basis of public health knowledge in the United States. Their failure to get them accepted was due to a lack of knowledge of the people's work habits, patterns of social interaction and belief system—all parts of the local culture.[1]

We have cited these examples of failures to introduce new ideas, not because we know of no successes, but because the problem is how to avoid failures. There are many Americans and other Westerners who deal successfully with people of other cultures, usually by means of good intuitive judgment, but there are equally large numbers who have not been able to surmount the culture barrier.

It is our belief that *the insights for cross-cultural interaction must be lifted above the level of intuitive judgment.* The brain surgeon must use his best judgment for each individual operation, but this judgment is based on thorough prior knowledge of the nature of the human body, the characteristics of infection, the uses of various drugs, and all the other aspects of medicine which make him an M.D. We believe that the social engineer—the government technician, the foundation representative, the missionary and the businessman—should also have all the knowledge that is available about the nature of human society and culture before he begins to administer new ideas, which constitute the medicine of social change.

The preceding examples of failures in introducing new ideas have been given merely to indicate the importance of cultural factors. The record of efforts in the last few decades indicates that without some knowledge of local customs and beliefs (the culture), most new ideas or techniques introduced into the developing countries by the developed ones will either fail or do more long-range harm than short-range good. The changes have to be integrated into the local culture in order to be considered truly successful. If the idea remains behind when the innovator leaves, the effort has been successful. The innovator not only needs to be a specialist in his field—agriculture, business, education, engineering, public health—but he also needs to develop the ability to make these specialties available to persons with customs and outlooks on life that differ from his own.

This manual attempts to assemble the *basic cultural factors* which should be understood for the successful introduction of new ideas or techniques. It will indicate some of the general principles that social scientists have learned in their study of *cultural change*. It cannot give the exact answers to specific problems, but it can be helpful as a guide in thinking out the problems of contact and cooperation with the people of the recipient countries. Its ultimate purpose is to stimulate the American who is going overseas as a change agent to be sensitive to cultural problems.

Because the innovator of new ideas is involved in diplomatic and human relations assignments as well as in teaching, even when this is informal, he requires more than merely his technical specialty to do the job successfully. He needs to prepare himself thoroughly for the contacts he will have with the different kinds of people who constitute the population in the area where he will work. Although he will be in contact with other foreigners—various kinds of technical aid specialists from many countries, missionaries, businessmen, and foreigners who have settled in the country—his main concern will be with the people of the nation to which he is bringing his special knowledge. To a large extent his dealings will be with government officials or the host elite. But ultimately he will be affecting the life of the common man, the rural villager, the poorer townsman and the member of the newly-emerging middle class. He must know a good deal of their way of life to deal with these people successfully. *Knowing the elite alone will not be enough.*

In addition to knowing as much as possible about the culture of the people in the host country, the change agent needs to have an understanding of the nature of culture contact in general: how and why people of different cultures borrow ideas from one another. He should also know something of the relations between the industrialized West and the underdeveloped nations of Asia, Africa, and Latin America during the last four hundred years, since many of the attitudes and administrative structures of these countries are a result of these experiences. He should be capable of recognizing the crucial factors of the culture change process which can spell success or failure in his own efforts to transfer new techniques. He should also learn to perceive what is possible for the local people, judged by the real conditions of their lives. And he should learn which approaches enlist their active cooperation and desire for assistance.

To bring about true lasting development, the innovator needs to distinguish between the froth of passing events and the deeper, underlying, more persistent habits and patterns of living that mark a way of life. All peoples have enduring institutional patterns that have continuity and are often carried down through many generations. These can survive modernizations, political upheavals, and the swings of fashion.

For instance, in Egypt, the posture farmers assume today in cutting grain (with a short-handled sickle) is the same as that depicted on the wall paintings in ancient Egyptian tombs; and, in India, the attitude of Hindus toward the cow is recognizable in the Vedas, the ancient sacred literature of the Hindus. Since then many dynasties and different forms of government have risen and fallen in both Egypt and India; now both are independent nations attempting to achieve standards of living approaching those of the West.

If an innovator wishes to introduce a new idea that will fit permanently into the local culture pattern, it needs to be reworked and adapted. The change will be accepted if it fits and is technically superior; but it will have to be cast into a form somewhat different from the original. The innovator must expect this and welcome it as a necessity for integrating the change into the culture.

Neither this book nor the social sciences on which it is based can give specific directions for solving the problems of each people and place, or for each specific kind of technical advance. There is no adequate body of facts about the life and habits of each of the diverse peoples of the world. Economic and social change is taking place all over the world— in many places quite rapidly; the local national customs and thought of one decade may be out of date the next. Moreover, the social sciences are rapidly increasing their knowledge in the field of applied technical change.

The main function of this book is to try to instill an approach, a sensitivity, an inventiveness, and a set of principles for the cultural solution of such problems. Primarily it can show the change agent his main challenge; to search out and find the local customs into which his innovations can best be blended. He already knows his professional specialty; to be a successful innovator, he must also learn something of the process of cultural change.

☐ **THE SOCIAL SCIENCES**

Knowledge about the different peoples of the world, their ways of living and thinking, is being gathered, evaluated, and analyzed by several scientific disciplines. No one of them covers all the necessary facts. Those most immediately concerned are the social (human) sciences:

1. *Anthropology,* particularly in the division known as *cultural anthropology,* in which we study the different peoples and cultures of the world, especially their total way of life.
2. *Sociology,* in which we study the forms and process of group life and social relationships, both statistically and through the analysis of institutions.
3. *Psychology,* particularly in the division of *social psychology,* in which we study the nature, role, learning process, and capabilities of human beings, together with the effects in behavior and attitude resulting from the individual's group membership.

Although the social sciences are vital for an understanding of peoples in the underdeveloped areas, they are, of course, not the only disciplines concerned with the study of man. *Economics, history* and *political science* concern themselves with specific kinds of human behavior; some knowledge of their contribution to the understanding of each cultural area is also vital. Anyone who wishes to understand the modern world must know something of the history, economics and political events that helped form the countries of Asia, Africa, and Latin America. But for a few exceptions, the usual curriculum offered by educational institutions in the United States and Europe is hardly sufficient for dealing with the world problems of today—certainly not enough for the persons trying to introduce new ideas.

The particular contribution of the social sciences is that of providing an understanding of how a society and culture function at local levels rather than considering only broad trends of development and change. The social sciences attempt to give a complete description of a culture rather than dealing only with a specific segment of behavior, such as economics or politics.

Anthropology was chosen as the science around which this manual was organized because it has concerned itself more than the others with the study of non-Western or pre-industrial peoples and with an understanding of the whole way of life of a people. Because of this concern with the whole way of life, the concepts of anthropology are more helpful in organizing the relevant data supplied by the other disciplines. Furthermore, because of its primary interest in the study of non-Western peoples, anthropology has worked out methods to compare diverse ways of life. The field procedures of anthropology have been developed for discovering and understanding non-Western ways of life quickly and directly.

☐   **ORGANIZATION OF THE MANUAL**

The manual is divided into seven parts, as follows:

Chapter I is an introduction to cultural problems in general.

Chapter II will provide a description of the concept of culture, man's unique achievement which was responsible for his dominance over all other animal species. This will include the effects of race, language, and environment on cultural progress, plus the conservatism, values and integration of all cultures.

Chapter III will treat unplanned changes in culture, a universal fact in man's cultural history.

Chapter IV will describe the major factors relevant to planned cultural change.

Chapter V will give a profile of what most underdeveloped areas have in common.

Chapter VI will outline American cultural values which the overseas change agent tends to take for granted but which, if understood, can help in his interaction with people who have different cultural values.

Finally, Chapter VII will discuss field problems of the innovator and social science research methods that can be adapted to his needs.

2

THE CONCEPT OF CULTURE

☐ **BIOLOGICAL DRIVES**

Man, like all other animals, has certain biological drives. In former years a great many instincts were thought to be a part of man's makeup but most instincts are now recognized as being the results of specific cultural training rather than innate biological characteristics of a given group of men, or of all men.

There are still wide-spread popular ideas based on the old theory. One of the most common is that a people are "naturally" lazy. Many white Americans regard American Indians as lazy because they often do not take the initiative to improve their farms or houses or to better themselves in the usual American manner. However, there is no good scientific evidence to indicate that the Indians would not work as hard as white Americans, were they interested in achieving the same goals. Their "laziness," where it occurs, is more a result of having lost their original culture values when they were overrun by American whites, and then not substituting the values of the whites. It is a matter of cultural change rather than any instinctive quality.

The same is true of other characteristics often attributed to people of non-Western culture when they are believed to be instinctively—or more commonly nowadays "naturally"—religious, or aggressive, or peaceful, or hardworking. Almost

12

always when the term "instinctively" or "naturally" is used to describe a human characteristic, it is a product of cultural training and is definitely subject to change.

Since man is an animal, he shares certain needs and characteristics with them. Those accepted by most anthropologists nowadays are quite basic and limited in number. These few drives, common to all animals, must be satisfied by all cultures. Five such basic needs are sustenance, rest, procreation, self-preservation, and—for man—social recognition. Man must provide food and drink for himself; he must rest periodically; he must reproduce his own kind; he must attempt to defend himself, and he must have social recognition from his fellows.

The way different cultures can control these different drives is endless, but in any culture some way must be found. There is a vast range of possible ways to satisfy the need of recognition. In a relatively rich, modern culture, such as that of the United States or Western Europe, a man will work hard in order to buy a large, expensive, new car; he will use his car not only as a means of transportation but also as a symbol of his status in the community. A man of a hill tribe in Southeast Asia, not being familiar with or able to afford such an expensive item, will nevertheless try to save enough from his meager resources to buy a pair of ivory ear plugs; he will pay the equivalent of thirty to forty dollars for them and will wear them to show others that he, too, is successful in terms of his own culture.

Procreation, the need to reproduce young, can also have a wide range of possibilities, established by cultural rules. There are cultures that permit considerable freedom in sexual conduct to women as well as men—before marriage as well as after. Many of the cultures of the Western Pacific islands have sexual codes of this sort. Other cultures, such as those of Hindu and Muslim India, are quite puritanical in their codes, particularly concerning women. Nevertheless, the begetting of babies is a central function of the male and female union in all cases and is so recognized by the culture, and arrangements are made that reward couples for having babies.

☐   MAN'S UNIQUE ACHIEVEMENT

Man begins on an animal base and has drives similar to other animals, but he has achieved an entirely new manner of adapting to life. Physical evolution has permitted other animals to develop specializations of a great variety and enabled different species to adapt themselves to many diverse kinds of environments. They have developed fins to swim with, wings to fly with, fangs and claws to kill with, and long, slim legs to make them swift-running. Different species have been able to adapt themselves to life at the bottom of the sea, near mountaintops, in lush rain forests, or in arid deserts.

But these changes in animal form have been physical specializations, making the particular animal well fitted for a certain type of life in a certain kind of environment. Moreover, they have required the animal to follow the kind of life its body has been built for. A lion could not convert itself into a vegetarian, nor could a deer convert itself into a meat eater. Man can, of course, change his dietary habits completely with no bodily change whatsoever.

Man also passed through evolutionary physical changes, but the end product we know today, *homo sapiens,* appeared on earth about 40,000 years ago and is an animal unspecialized in body, though with an elaboration of posture, brain, hand, eye, and tongue. These changes have permitted him to develop a new kind of adaptation to living, one that seems more successful than the physical specializations of the other animals. Man learned to speak and make symbols to communicate his ideas freely; he also learned to make tools in place of the specialized body parts of the other animals. He has learned to cross water easily without fins, to race over land without being swift-running, to fly without wings, and to fight without fangs or claws. He became a tool-using animal with the ability to communicate and build from one invention to the next and to pass on information from one generation to the next. Man's unique achievement was the development of systems of learned behavior which in the broadest use of the term are what we call *culture*.

☐ CULTURE IS LEARNED

Culture is the sum total of what human beings learn in common with other members of the group to which they belong. An adult has learned the ways of the people who reared him and taught him what they knew, most of which they had learned from their elders. And although toolmaking was perhaps the primary kind of specifically human behavior, and still remains central in human activities, culture includes much more. It includes all kinds of learning and behavior, the customs that men have developed for living together in groups, the ideas they have of deity and the supernatural, the beliefs they have of what is noble and good.

The habit of shaking hands to establish a cordial relationship with a stranger is a part of the Western cultural repertory, though it is not natural to the Asian whose culture has taught him to bow at the waist, or to hold his hands palms together near his face and bow his head slightly. Such customs are so deeply ingrained in the individual that he is often not aware that they have significance in only his own culture. For instance, one insignia used to indicate American aid overseas is a pair of clasped hands; to the American who devised it, this signified brotherly friendship. To most Asian villagers, however, clasped hands is a kind of greeting which they associate with dominant whites, since they learned it from their colonial masters in the last two or three centuries.

Beliefs about the supernatural are a part of culture. A Christian of the West may believe that his deity is concerned only with the soul and has nothing to do with bodily health, which is a matter to be tended by secular medical specialists. In most non-Western societies, however, supernatural power is believed to be possessed by certain individuals who can make others ill and whose influences have to be counteracted by ritual means. This, too, is a cultural difference.

Cultural behavior is learned and passed on from one generation to the next; this is of vital importance in the concept of culture. Other animals can learn individually from experience and can pass on a fraction of what they have learned to their young, but only by demonstration or in an immediate situation. Carnivorous animals do take their young out on their first hunts and do teach them hunting methods. Mother foxes are known to bring animals that they have caught and mutilated to their dens; this is to permit the young cubs to kill under their surveillance. They will also take their young out and show them where to find and how to catch different kinds of mice. The young imitate their parents; but they lack man's great gift—symbolic language.

Man alone can pass on to his young information and knowledge about situations before they are encountered. By using words that stand for the things themselves, a fox with a symbolic language could explain to the young cubs where to go and what to do to find and catch gophers. Only man can thus simplify and organize the experimentation of his young with the world. He can pass on information and ideas from the persons who passed it on to him, persons whom he has never seen, information gathered through time when he did not live. Man is the "time-binder." He is not limited to the present like other animals, but has the experience of the past through his culture; he can even foresee the future by means of his science.

Most human behavior is thus learned; it is not innate. An American child of American parents who spends his life in India, with no contact with Americans, grows up to be culturally Indian. In language, motives, ideals, even in the way he walks and holds himself, he is like other Indians, showing the behavior and thought of those who reared him. Thus he grows up an Indian, regardless of his origin, although he remains as blond and blue-eyed as the parents he never saw.

In the same way, an American Negro may look physically like the forest villagers of the Congo or Dahomey who are his ancestral kin, but he has nothing in common with them except his appearance. His culture is American, which he shares with all others reared in America. The American melting pot is indeed one of the best indications of the power of learned behavior, because people from many parts of the world and of many physical types have been absorbed into American culture.

☐   **CULTURE AND RACE**

In a basic physical sense it is true that *all men are one* and that *differences between groups do not exist.* All men presently living and all who have lived for the past 40,000 years belong to one single species. All men can interbreed freely with the women of any other group—one of the main criteria for establishing a single species.

Yet groups of people differ in appearance in different parts of the world, and often even in the same region. In America, Negroes and whites have basic differences in their appearance. If a person boarded a plane in New York City, without knowing his destination, and landed first in Accra, Ghana, then later in Taipei, Taiwan, he would notice basic differences in the physical appearance of the people milling about the two airports.

Men have long been aware of the variations in physical appearance between different groups. In the 19th century and early 20th century, physical anthropologists attempted to subdivide the peoples of the world on the basis of their physical appearance. They used a great variety of traits of which the most common were stature, body build, head shape, nose shape, breast shape, hair texture and quantity, hair color, skin color and eye color.

The idea of "race" was first applied to the large groups of people who were easily recognizable from one another and who were native to separate parts of the world: the Caucasoids (whites) in Europe, the Negroids in Africa, and the Mongoloids in East Asia. There were, however, large numbers of people who did not fit these categories well; also there were considerable distinctions within some of the groups. The people of India were more like Europeans than any other people, though they were not very "white."

The term "white," incidentally, is one of the worst descriptive terms ever devised, since no group of people or individuals are truly white in color. What is normally called "white" is a variation of pink or light tan. However, the term has been inculcated so deeply in people's thinking all over the world that, even in the countries of brown-skinned men, Europeans and Americans are regarded as "white." That is what their schoolmasters taught them. Because it is so commonly used, we will use the term, "white," in this manual; but it will refer to Europeans or people of European ancestry—a cultural rather than a racial designation.

The Negroes are thought to be characteristic of Africa, but a large number of a somewhat different kind of Negroes live in the Southwest Pacific—the Melanesians. Also, there are very tall Negroes in East Africa and extremely short ones, the Pygmies, in Central Africa. Moreover, the Caucasoids of Northern Europe are different in appearance from southern Italians and Spaniards. Consequently smaller groups of people —such as Nordics, Alpines, Mediterraneans, Pygmies and Forest Negroes—have been termed "sub-races."

The problem of physical differences was accentuated in the 18th and 19th centuries, during the period of European colonization and slave traffic. The people that were being enslaved, colonized, or exploited were of a wide variety of physical types; but almost all of them were darker skinned than the Europeans. Although the exploitation of these people was economic, the treatment accorded them required some moralistic explanation. Biological and "racial" inferiority was invoked as justification; that is, the dark-skinned people, whether Negroes, American Indians, or East Indians, were claimed to be physically inferior to the Anglo-Saxons and other Europeans.

Men have been exploited by other men, usually through slavery, ever since the dawn of civilization; but racial differences were not always used as a justification. The early civilizations came closer to recognizing that differences between groups of men were primarily cultural. These early civilizations divided people into categories of "citizens" and "barbarians." Barbarians were simply people who did not know the civilized ways of doing things and their physical characteristics were irrelevant.

The doctrine of racial inferiority was first used to justify European and Anglo-Saxon supremacy over dark-skinned people; in its most recent, vicious form it appeared in the Nazi theory of the Aryan master race. In this instance, it was not even applied to a distinct physical group but to a nation, Germany, that had a variety of physical types.

A reverse tendency has appeared in the world in the last twenty years, but cultural differences are still confused with racial ones. Since achieving independence, the people once lumped together by "white" racists have now reacted and developed a milder form of "white" racism. That is, they sometimes act together under the assumption that colored people have common goals against the light-skinned Europeans, Americans, South Africans, Australians and New Zealanders. Culturally, a politician from Ghana has little more in common with an Indonesian or an East Indian than he has with an Argentinian or a Greek, but he does share with the former a common history of exploitation by Europeans and the description of being "colored." The Communists, particularly in Asia, recognize the utility of this idea and encourage it wherever they can. Russian Communists cannot, however, carry it too far since they are racially akin to Western Europeans.

Racial or sub-racial classifications based on physical characteristics have been largely changed or abandoned by physical anthropologists in the past twenty years. Although physical differences exist, the idea of race is an abstraction. No individual completely fits the characteristics described by the early theorists; instead, there is an endless gradation of types. For instance, the Nordics have been described as blond, blue-eyed, tall, with narrow heads, and living in Northern Europe. In fact, this ideal type rarely occurs. Instead, one finds blond, blue-eyed, short people with round heads; and tall people with narrow heads, but with brown hair and eyes; and all the other combinations possible with this number of physical traits. Also, many of these physical traits may change with diet and better living conditions. Body build and head shape are known to have changed in immigrants moving to the United States. This means that some traits are not completely hereditary but are influenced by the environment as well.

Nevertheless, men do differ in a general way. East Indians can usually be distinguished from the Northern Chinese, and Swedes from Central African Negroes. To understand culture, it is important to know the relationship of these physical characteristics to the mental abilities of the different groups. This was the crux of the racist theories. The differences in appearance between Negroes and Anglo-Saxons were merely a means of separating people visually. The important thing to the racists was to prove that the darker people were inferior in innate mental ability.

One of the most common ways used to indicate this inferiority has been differences in scores on intelligence tests. In general, non-whites have made lower scores on these tests. In the United States, most such testing of non-whites has been done with Negroes. The main difficulty with intelligence tests has been that they do not measure innate ability as much as what people have learned; and what they have learned is more a product of their environment than of their potential ability. Negroes have had poorer schooling, poorer opportunities for advancement, and have been generally discriminated against socially; so they have often learned less than whites. There is no evidence that a Negro, given equal opportunity, cannot do anything that a white can do.

Anthropological research has shown that *there are no groups of people in the world that differ systematically in any kind of mental endowment*. To the contrary, the evidence indicates that all groups of men have about the same range of distribution of human abilities. The majority of leaders of men have appeared among whites in recent centuries only because the whites have had more opportunity—their cultures have been in a leadership position. If we consider why no Negro Columbus discovered America, a simple explanation is that no African cultures then had ships capable of making such a trip. Inborn intelligence or ability of any kind has proved so difficult to disentangle from the effects of education, opportunity, and social environment that we should no longer ascribe the achievements of any people to their physical characteristics.

One of the best arguments against the theory of innate superiority of one group over others is provided by a brief look at man's cultural history. In the last 400 years European whites have been in the ascendancy in technical and political developments, in progress achieved through the industrial revolution and in expansion into the other parts of the world. However, before this time the torch of civilization had been carried by one dark-skinned group of people after another.

The Egyptians, the Sumerians (of present-day Iraq), the Hindus, the Chinese, and the Arabs developed mighty civilizations and contributed significantly to the base on which the industrial revolution of Europe was built. There is a long roster of inventions and innovations derived from these peoples that we use today. Some of the more important ones are: the domestication of animals and plants; the wheel; the smelting of bronze, iron and steel; the solar calendar; the zero and a place numeral system; irrigation systems; gunpowder; writing systems; and the printing press.

The American Indians, who have so often been written off as "barbarians," have also contributed a great deal. Their main achievement was in the domestication of plants, and it is estimated that today two-thirds of the world's production of crops is of plants originally domesticated by the Indians; the most important are corn, beans, cotton, and tobacco.

Negro Africa has often been cited as the continent where little in the development of man took place. Although in recent centuries it has not been a center of civilization, it now seems probable that the first faltering steps toward man-ness were made in this region about a million years ago. The South African "ape-men" now seem to be the first creatures who developed culture, probably inventing the first tools and the first symbolic language—both prime necessities for all later advancements in man's culture. In sum, the differences in cultural development throughout the world have been influenced very little by the physical characteristics of a people.

Even if groups of men are difficult to characterize according to their physical appearance, and even if no mental inferiority has ever been proved, a notion of race continues to exist in the world. Over the centuries, most old, inbred populations have developed recognizable types that can be tied to a common culture. They tend to develop groups that look alike, perhaps of several standard types. For example, in Ireland, where florid redheads, swarthy "black Irishmen," and blue-eyed, white-skinned brunettes (the "colleen" type) are all common, a Negro, an ash blond, or a Japanese would look different and "un-Irish." If such physical characterisics are tied to cultural differences, they can be used to distinguish people. This is what happened to the Negroes in the United States; at first they were identified with slavery and later became an underprivileged farm labor class.

Some modern politicians in India tend to regard themselves as racial brothers with Negro Africans; this is a part of the commonness they promoted by forming an Afro-Asian bloc. The end purpose was political and economic cooperation, but physical similarities (though not very great) were used to accomplish this end. The Indians of India have little other relationship with Africans except this remote political and economic tie, so no other attitude toward them has developed. On the other hand, on the island of Trinidad in the West Indies, where Africans were first brought as slaves and Indians later came as indentured laborers, there is a considerable amount of economic and social friction between the two groups and they stress differences in physical characteristics. In both instances the same peoples have two different attitudes because the economic and social conditions are different.

Racial feeling enters the scene when a people excludes from its group persons of other physical types and assigns inferior and superior social rank on this basis. Racial customs then become a part of the local culture. Such racial attitudes are learned in some cultures, never learned in others. In New Zealand, the native people (the Maori), who were subjected by British immigrants, now live on a plane of equality with them. Hawaii has often been noted as the "melting pot of the Pacific"; people of American, Japanese, Filipino, Chinese, and Hawaiian ancestry live together there with no ranking of superior or inferior groups. Color bars still exist in the world, but they are becoming steadily fewer as the colonial world shrinks and as the Western concept of "inalienable rights" spreads.

Attitudes toward groups of people will vary from country to country and though they may be related to physical traits, the bases for distinction are usually economic or social. The American overseas will have to learn the bases of distinction for the country he is in.

In countries of Southeast Asia like Laos, Thailand, and Burma, the local population is normally divided into two groups—the hill tribes and the dominant people of the valleys, the Lao, Thai, and Burmese. There are also significant populations of more recent immigrants, particularly the East Indians and Chinese. Although the local people may note some physical differences between the groups (Chinese with the lightest skins, hill tribes with the darkest), the primary distinction is by culture and language. The Thai, Chinese and hill tribes of Thailand all have languages of their own, their religious beliefs are different, and their social and economic customs are different.

In other countries, the distinctions have no racial basis at all and may even lack language differences. The Muslims and Hindus of North Central India cannot be distinguished by race and they speak the same basic language, even though their alphabets (Arabic and Devanagari) are different. In this case all that separates them is a difference in religious beliefs and practices, plus the social practices derived from these.

In Latin America, there are people of Negro, Amerindian, and European ancestry and there are some cultural differences separating these groups. However, people in that part of the world are most often divided according to their social and economic position. In general, the whites are in the better classes, but when people of Amerindian or Negro ancestry achieve the same education and wealth, they are accepted as equals by the whites.[2] Thus, even where the term Indian or Negro is used, it signifies the social status of the individual more than his ancestry.

There is no necessary correlation between race, language, nationality, or culture. A situation can exist where two racial types share the same language, nationality and culture, as with American Negroes and whites. On the other hand, two groups of people may have the same nationality but differ in race, language, and culture—as with the whites and the dark-skinned Bantu of the Union of South Africa. A people can be of the same racial type and share the same spoken language, yet differ in nationality and in some aspects of culture—for example, religion, as with the majority of people in India and Pakistan. All the other combinations are possible and occur in different parts of the world.

It is *culture,* not physical differences, that defines social differences. The American overseas should be prepared to recognize, understand, and work within a framework of the distinctions that the local people enforce upon one another. Some system of group distinction and subordination is present in every culture; it must be learned in its own terms and against its own history.

☐   **ENVIRONMENT**

All animals except man have managed to cope with their environment by means of physical changes. New surroundings, say a move to the Arctic, demands that the animal species evolve a breed with dense fur, thick down, or blubber. To the best of our knowledge, only through genetic change—an irreversible process that requires a long period of time—can such an evolution occur. This means that a particular adaptation does not enable an animal to make a greater variety of other adaptations. If it has adjusted to Arctic conditions, like a polar bear or walrus, it will be completely unable to survive under desert conditions.

The human animal, man, developed a completely new method of responding to his environment—a method that was neither one-way nor dependent on genetic mutations, namely, culture. *Culture is man's unique way of adapting to environment.* Culture provides man with many alternative solutions to problems of survival, teachable to all beings capable of speech and human customs.

In moving to the Arctic, man, too, must solve the problem of cold temperatures, but the solutions will vary, according to the cultural knowledge available. Man's answer to cold weather is warm clothing, warm houses, various heating devices, and warm vehicles; these are a part of his technological knowledge, not changes in his physical make-up. The Eskimo, the Chukchi of Siberia, the Norwegians, and now the modern Euro-Americans have all successfully met this challenge of the Arctic in different ways. The Eskimo invented snowblock and semi-subterranean houses; the Chukchi, drawstring felt bags to be used as tents; the Norwegians, moss-chinked log cabins with stoves; and the modern Americans, buildings of steel and stone, heated by furnaces.

Such types of cultural adaptation are cumulative. Each people can build on the knowledge of the previous generation, or can borrow ideas from neighbors. The knowledge is not transmitted through man's genes but through his intelligence, his eyes and ears, and his manual skills. The possibilities of adaptation have increased so much through the development of culture that man has been able to cover the earth regardless of climatic conditions. By the 20th century, the only regions of the world that had not been claimed as habitations for man were the Antarctic, the tops of the highest mountains, and the depths of the sea. Even in the mountains, man has been able to work out satisfactory living conditions up to 13,000 feet, and he has now increased his activity in the Antarctic.

Man not only adapts to specific environments; he also

changes them. While animals may change their environment to a limited degree (beavers building dams to create artificial lakes), they have accomplished nothing that is comparable to the influence of man. Man has burned the vegetation of the prairies, denuded forests on a continental scale, changed the courses of rivers, created mammoth new lakes, turned fertile land into deserts, and now is even experimenting with producing rainfall. There are areas in Asia that are believed to have been under cultivation so long and so intensively that no one knows what the original wild vegetation was.

Man's ability to cope with environmental differences has been very successful, yet he has not been able to divorce himself completely from environmental limitations. A specific environment permits certain possibilities and limits others. In a climate as harsh as that of the Arctic or of the Kalahari Desert of South Africa, people with simple technologies have been able to work out successful specialized methods of survival. In both areas agriculture is next to impossible, or at least very difficult, and an exclusive dependence on hunting and gathering wild foods does not permit a civilized kind of life.

On the other hand, the environment does not enforce a particular level of cultural development. It limits the possibilities of adaptation, though they become greater as technological development becomes more advanced. In the Kalahari Desert the Bushman barely manages to eke out an existence hunting wild animals and gathering wild plants, yet the same land could be made fertile with an adequate irrigation system. In Alaska, the Eskimo managed by hunting sea mammals and caribou; today, by importing the industrial technology of the mid-20th century, cities have been built there and resources such as minerals, fish, and timber exploited far more fully than was possible for the Eskimo. In a Southeast Asian country such as Thailand, the people in the lowlands, with a technology and social organization permitting them to dig drainage and irrigation canals, can exploit the vast, rich river bottoms. Meanwhile the tribal people in the hills eke out a much poorer existence, cutting down forest patches and planting a dry rice that produces much less than the lowland's wet rice.

The same environment can support a variety of cultures and economies, depending on the technological knowledge of the people. In the semi-arid plateaus of Arizona, one finds five different sub-cultures side by side, despite the same terrain and climate—Navajo shepherds, Hopi gardeners, Spanish-American villagers, Mormon farmers, and Anglo-American ranchers. Conversely, a uniform culture may cover both mountains and plains, as in most of Western Europe.

Environment conditions culture, but does not make it. In the underdeveloped countries, where there are mountains, savannas, tropical forests, oceanic islands and deserts, there are many different environments. In different ways and according to their level of technical knowledge, the local peoples have adapted to them successfully enough for survival. Since, however, their technical knowledge is not as advanced as that of the United States and other developed nations, the environment limits them more than it does us.

North Americans who go to tropical countries can easily read more influence into environmental limitations than they truly merit. Going from their own temperate climate to regions where the heat is considerable during most of the year, and where the people seem to work less than in the United States or Europe, it is easy to conclude that it is the climate that has retarded cultural development. The Americans themselves often feel less energetic and attribute this to the stultifying effect of the heat.

Moreover, if one maps the developed regions of the world, all of them with one exception (Hawaii) are found in the cooler latitudes.[3] This seems to indicate that the climate, at least the temperature, is directly responsible for technical development. But this is not necessarily true. One can just as easily argue that the people of the underdeveloped countries work less hard because their countries are underdeveloped and there is far less reason to exert oneself. The people with opportunities for advancement in such countries, the elite class, very often work as hard as any American businessman. Also, there are different work rhythms in hot areas that may be more suitable for such areas than those of the temperate regions. During the growing seasons the farmers usually work quite hard. A siesta or rest period in the middle of the day is probably quite sensible. The early morning and late afternoon are much cooler and there are plenty of overseas Americans who have learned the utility of the midday rest period.

In addition to a possible real need to adapt to the climatic conditions of the tropics, an American may feel less energetic because of trying to work according to the same schedule used at home, and because of trying to adapt to difficult work situations. In contrast, Americans and Europeans who have lived for many years in the tropics ordinarily find it no more difficult to work than do their counterparts at home, at least insofar as the climate is concerned.

The question still remains as to why the underdeveloped countries are almost all in the warm zones, while the developed ones are in cool areas. In our use of the term, "development" refers to events of the last 400 years only, the period of the industrial revolution and European expansion. Applied in this sense, all the developed countries of today with one exception (Japan), are places where the majority of the population is of European ancestry, or where European colonists were permanent settlers rather than colonial masters exploiting the native population.

In Anglo-America (Canada and the United States), which is classified as developed, the native Indian population constitutes only a fraction of the total. The three countries of South America that are classified as developed (Argentina, Chile, and Uruguay) have populations of predominantly Spanish ancestry; the sparse Indian population has long since been eliminated or absorbed. In one country of Africa classified as developed, the Union of South Africa, the majority of the population is non-white; the white minority came there as permanent settlers and established a double standard of living, one for whites and one for non-whites.

The only Asian and Oceanic areas classified as developed

are Japan, Hawaii, New Zealand and Australia.[4] Like the United States and Canada, New Zealand and Australia are countries where European immigrants came and set up an economic and political system similar to that of their homeland. The native populations are insignificant. Modern Hawaii, though it has a widely diverse population, was developed primarily under the impetus of Americans and its economy was integrated with that of the United States. This leaves only one country developed by non-Europeans, Japan.

The significance of this distribution is that the Europeans who resettled chose areas of the world that were similar to their native countries, areas for which their own technology was well suited. If the industrial revolution had taken place in India or the Middle East, the developed areas of the world today might have been those in the warm zones.

This present day view of development is a short range one, that of the last 400 years. If one takes a long view of man's cultural history, that of the last 8,000 years, most of civilized life was centered in the warmer regions of the earth, if not in the full tropics—in the Middle East, India, Southeast Asia, China, and tropical or sub-tropical areas of the Americas. The same basic inventions, devised by the darker-skinned peoples, occurred in these areas. Europe achieved very little of importance until the close of the Middle Ages; the achievements that did take place with the coming of the industrial revolution were built on the base erected by peoples of the warmer zones during the previous 7,500 years. The difference between the developed nations and the underdeveloped ones is no more a matter of climatic differences than it is one of racial differences; it is, rather, a product of cultural development.

☐   **LANGUAGE**

Spoken language and culture are inseparable. Intelligent beings might have invented some other basic form of communication, but man has devised only this one; we cannot

conceive of even the most primitive forms of cultural life
without it. We do not know of any people without a spoken
language.

Most simply defined, language is a system of sounds in
which each sound is arbitrarily made to stand for an idea.
The idea of a horse may be indicated by the sounds "horse,"
cheval, caballo, ghodaa, or *maa;* yet, without being in its
presence, a man can discuss this creature with anyone who
understands the meaning of the same sounds and who speaks
his language. Man transmits almost all of his ideas through
language; a very important result is that he thus passes on his
cultural knowledge to the next generation. The continuity and
growth of culture are therefore directly dependent on language. All new ideas are verbalized and incorporated into a
language; so it also becomes a vehicle of change.

A language is inextricably linked with all aspects of a
culture. Nothing more clearly distinguishes one culture from
another than its language. We sometimes confuse writing systems with the spoken language of the people; otherwise we
could say that the infallible sign of a separate culture is a
separate language and the inevitable result of a separate
language is a separate culture. For example, England, the
United States, and Ireland all use English today as a literary
written language, but they speak British, American, and the
"brogue" (when not Gaelic). They are in fact three separate,
though related, cultures. It is the spoken, not the written language that is basic.

Different writing forms can make languages seem completely different, although they are merely separate dialects.
The people of northern India and West Pakistan speak a
mutually intelligible language, Hindustani, yet their writing
systems are quite distinctive. The Pakistanis use an Arabic-
derived script, Urdu, while the Indians use a Sanscrit-derived
writing system. The spoken language changes more quickly
than the written form and represents the culture much more
closely. Writing systems are very important in modern life,
particularly because they enable men to keep ideas in an un-

changing recorded form over long periods of time. The growth of scientific ideas has rested largely on this development.

Due to our high rate of literacy, it is easy for us to over-emphasize the importance of a writing system. A system of writing is merely a technique applied to a spoken language in order to give it visual form. It does not in itself make that language superior to one that is not written. A culture with a language that is not written, or in which the majority of people is illiterate, does not suffer so much because the language is inferior but because communication between the people is so much more difficult.

Language is sometimes singled out as an explanation for the retardation of cultures. Does this mean that some languages are incapable of transmitting the ideas necessary for modern life? Based on the research of the last fifty years, linguists and anthropologists have concluded that the potential of communicating ideas exists in all languages. In a less developed culture, there may be difficulty in expressing ideas because of a paucity of vocabulary and because there has been no need to have words for modern scientific ideas, since such ideas have not been incorporated into the culture. Languages become elaborate when there is cultural need for elaboration. It has been said that generalizations were not possible in primitive languages. This is a relative matter. If there is a cultural need to generalize or to specify, it will be reflected in the language.

For instance, Eskimo has a large number of specific terms to describe snow, rather than one general term as in English. This makes sense when one realizes that snow in different forms is of vital importance to these people. A blizzard spelling deprivation or isolation, a precipitation heralding warmer air and the advent of spring, traveling by sled, building houses, using snowshoes—each of these is associated with a different kind of snow. Another instance comes from a completely different type of zone, the desert. The Somali nomads who depend for their livelihood on camel, goat, and sheep herding must know their terrain well; consequently they have separate words for thirty or more different types of land, which to an outsider looks monotonously the same.[5] For devices that they may see but that are not intimately associated with their lives, such as an airplane, such people will have but a single generalized word. On the other hand, a modern American boy has a great variety of words to describe airplanes, the different kinds as well as many different parts of the machine; while to him the desert is just the desert, and snow is indicated by only one word.

Each culture reflects what is of value to them in their language. But languages can change rapidly by inventing new words and by borrowing them outright from other cultures when the need arises.

People overseas often wonder about the relative difficulty of learning languages—whether some are intrinsically more difficult than others. All languages are learned by all normal children with reasonable proficiency by the time they are six years old. This has nothing to do with the child's ancestry. Although a Chinese child learns Chinese and an Indian child Hindustani, this is by coincidence. The Indian child would learn Chinese just as fluently if that was the language he heard as he grew up. It is reported that the Indian emperor, Akbar, when told by early Christian missionaries that the original language of mankind was Hebrew, isolated a group of children where they could hear no language spoken. He wished to find out if they would speak Hebrew! The nurses used sign language in the presence of the children. When the children were grown up they also used sign language.

A language with a greater similarity in the sound system and grammar to the speaker's original language should prove easier to learn than one less similar, but none are insuperable. To say that one "does not have an ear for languages" is not an explanation. Some people can learn languages better than others, but the difference is usually lack of application rather than lack of "ear." Anyone overseas need only look at the missionaries. They assume from the beginning that they will learn the local language and almost without exception they do. They have learned what some other overseas Americans have also learned—that there is no tool as important for understanding another culture and for getting along with the local people as an understanding of their language.

□ **TECHNOLOGY**

As indicated in the section above on environment, the technology of a people is a major factor in their way of adjusting to their environment. Language and technology are the two most basic characteristics of human culture. Which came first is not known, but it is assumed that the first crude attempts to make tools coincided with the first attempts at symbolic languages. The one sure index of human advancement is in the technological field. Different religious beliefs, ways of organizing human relationships, and systems of economy have been developed by men during their million year history, and it is possible that there has been some progressive change in these fields of conduct; but the one incontrovertible form of progress has been in the field of technology. It is possible to argue the relative merits of arranged marriage versus free choice of spouses; but it is not possible to argue the relative merits of a stone axe as compared to one made of steel, or of a bow and arrow as compared to a gun. The steel axe and the gun obviously do the job better, and the simplest demonstration proves this.

There are no people in the world who do not recognize the obvious utility of improved technological methods or devices. A system of political organization or a new religious belief may well be resisted, but people can recognize the obvious utility of improved technological methods or devices. In rare instances, superior technology may be rejected if its adoption would challenge the culture. Usually, however, people are impelled to adopt a technical improvement, if they have the opportunity to understand it and the means to acquire it. Metal implements and guns make good examples, though there are innumerable other ones.

There are no known people in the world who have refused

to acquire such items once they were made practicably available. The advantages of metal vessels over pottery jars, or over bamboo, basketry, or leather containers are too obvious to ignore. And the only reason that many people in the underdeveloped countries do not have guns is because they cannot afford to buy them or because the government restricts their ownership.

Quite often people have adopted technical devices superior to those they had before, but ultimately detrimental to their culture. Because of the technical superiority of the device, they failed to weigh the cultural loss. The Maori of New Zealand are reported to have decimated their own people in intertribal warfare once they obtained guns, which they had sought most eagerly.[6] In Australia, a whole culture fell to pieces simply because the people adopted steel axes to replace those made of stone. In this instance, the rituals, trading relationships with other tribes, and the social position of older men depended on their possession of stone axes. When steel axes became available through white missionaries, the urge to replace the stone axes was too strong to resist; all of the tribe who had the opportunity acquired them. They had acquired a better implement for cutting wood but the ritual life, the trading relationships, and the prestige of older men disappeared. The culture ultimately disintegrated because the social and religious life of the people became so weakened.[7]

Of course, there are sometimes new ideas of a political, social, or religious nature that ultimately cause a culture to perish; but these are often rejected because they are recognized to be harmful, or at least to have no immediately obvious utility. Although the Maori so quickly adopted the guns provided by the Englishmen, they were by no means as interested in the donors' political ideas, and even fought against the British with the same guns. And the Australians showed no great interest in Christianity when they sought steel axes from the missionaries.

Because technology is so basic to the survival of a culture, it is the kind of activity in which men show the most "rational" behavior. Rational, objective knowledge is necessary for even the most primitive kinds of technical effort. In order to plant rice and millet, a peasant farmer must know an exact technique. He must know when the rain will fall, how to prepare the fields, which fields to use, which kind of grain to use, how to irrigate, and how to deal with an endless number of other details necessary for a successful harvest. This is not to say that he will not also use ritual to help bring on tardy rains or drive away insect pests. No, his ideas of the supernatural, as well as his social relationships, will complicate and temper his "rationality." But the solid base of his technology will be practical. It was indeed this practicality which enabled him to work out his successful adaptation to his environment.

☐ **ECONOMY**

Since from the earliest times culture has been in the hands of a social animal, one who lives in groups, there has always been a need for some kind of distribution system, provision of services, and division of labor. This is what in simplest terms we call an *economy*. The complexity of the society, which is based largely on the level of the technology, will mainly determine the complexity of the economy and the forms it will take.

A people with a simple hunting and gathering technology will have very little surplus or variety of goods to distribute; they will have no need for individual ownership of land, specialized workers, true money, markets, and a host of other economic features we tend to take for granted. Even agricultural peasant societies, which form the majority of the people in the underdeveloped countries, will lack some features of modern Western economy. They may have individual ownership of land and some specialized workers, and they will have money; but they may lack markets, the concept of an hourly wage for labor given, the profit motive which we ordinarily consider so basic, and they may base many of their economic relationships on kinship. The differences, however, are relative, not absolute.

Land will be claimed by someone in even the most primitive societies. Usually people who depend on hunting and gathering for their subsistence will regard the band of people who stay together while traveling around the territory as the land-holding unit. There will be division of labor everywhere. The people with the simplest technologies will have the least elaboration, usually a difference of work only between men and women. The peasant societies will be made up mainly of farmers but they will have some artisans in their villages. Moreover, they will have the products of city specialists available and even some products of the world economy. In Southeast Asia, in very remote tribal areas in the hills, where the people live almost completely within a subsistence economy, the tribesmen wear loincloths, file their teeth to a point, and distend their ear lobes by heavy ivory plugs; but they will light their hand-rolled cheroots with cheap Japanese cigarette lighters or don thin pieces of plastic material as raincoats.

Much of the economic behavior of non-Western people may not appear rational to us, mainly because no clear-cut profit motive is apparent. We can better understand such behavior if, instead of the idea of immediate profit, we substitute the idea of reward. There can be many kinds of reward other than immediate financial gain without abandoning the idea of individual self-interest. Man has need for food, clothing, housing, and reproduction, and these are primary; but they do not have to be immediately or individually met. All peoples are aware of the need for long-term insurance and of the long-run disadvantages of immediate, individual gains.

One of the most common methods by which primitive people manage this is to encourage the idea of generosity and even of conspicuous giving. Hunting and gathering peoples with primitive technologies, such as the Eskimo, the Bushmen of South Africa, and the Semang of Malaya tend to share their products of the chase and the roots and berries they gather. Since they have no good methods of storage or of accumulating capital that can be liquidated in time of need, their economic insurance is the good will of their neighbors. Each family may primarily be looking out for itself but they get their reward and insurance through generosity. By giving generously, they not only eventually receive benefits of a material nature, but they obtain prestige and consideration as big men—commodities that can also be cashed in, as most successful modern politicians know.

Many primitive peoples, such as the Maori of New Zealand or the Northwest Coast Indians of Canada, used to indulge in elaborate feasts for the same purpose. To outsiders the feasts may have looked more wasteful than anything else, but the feast givers were gaining prestige and followers. This kind of behavior differs only in degree from that of the politician of a newly independent country in Asia or Africa who gives a big meal to peasants who come in to vote, or the American businessman who gives a case of whiskey or a box of cigars to all his clients on Christmas.

The peasant societies of the world often depend on kinship relationships as their form of economic insurance. A man is expected to stand behind his family and relatives, who are usually more numerous than those of a Western family. Young men are helped by the older men; but they in turn are expected to help their younger brothers and sisters, and more distant relatives. The family will rise, stand, or fall as a unit. It is, in a way, a primitive insurance corporation. It makes sense in such types of culture, although it may create problems when Western ideas of economy are brought into the picture.

In particular, an individual profit motive will cause difficulties. On numerous occasions men in non-Western societies have refused technical improvements because their acceptance would merely increase their work; more wealth would mean more relatives to support.

In societies where kinship is strong, people also expend a considerable amount of their wealth on family ceremonies, particularly marriage. This is a part of the whole picture. The binding together of different families through marriage is vital if kinship relations are to be maintained, and the ceremonial and financial aspects must be treated seriously. The ceremonies and financial exchanges are the cement. Where such economic behavior is considered as a method of insurance that is more necessary than in the relatively affluent West, it should not be condemned until something better is introduced and integrated into the culture.

Even in the West we are not psychologically at ease to work for nothing more than the immediate profit motive. The growth of insurance buying in the United States has been very great in recent years. An insurance policy is mainly designed to provide the security that immediate profits alone do not insure.

Another important form of human endeavor which is not purely "economic" is that expended in ritual and religious efforts. In Latin America, the Buddhist countries of Southeast Asia, Hindu India, and the Muslim world, people expend considerable amounts of effort and money on fiestas, fetes, *bouns*, pilgrimages, and lesser religious events. In Laos the easiest way to motivate the ordinary people to community effort is through religious festivals. On one occasion the Prince of Champassak, upon visiting his capital just before a religious fete, noticed the great efforts the people had put into renovating the area. He remarked to one of the authors who had been trying to do community development work in the locality, "If we could only get the Lao people to work every day as they do for fetes, we would have a very progressive nation."

Because a fete or fiesta has the elements of a county fair where everyone has a good time, it has considerable social importance in countries where entertainment facilities are limited. Since the people are working and spending money for religious ends, they must be receiving an important uneconomic reward—establishing good relations with their gods or saints, a need even Westerners will not deny, though they may consider religious and secular affairs as separate kinds of activity. In evaluating such "uneconomic" activities among non-Western people, it is important to consider their function in the total culture and possible alternative forms of behavior.

☐ SOCIAL ORGANIZATION

Because they live together in groups, men need to organize their relationships and activities between one another. Each people has its own conventions, social arrangements, and moral and ethical codes to govern their dealings with one another. There are at least three major institutions through which men have organized these relationships, though there are varying emphases on different sections of the three, according to the technological advancement of the culture.

First and foremost is the principle of *kinship,* upon which the very primitive people depend the most, and the most advanced people the least. This is the system of responsibilities toward relatives, and rights relied upon from relatives; it is derived from the basic human institution of marriage, the uniting of two unrelated people to produce a third. This institution is universal among all peoples; its main function is to bind together larger numbers of people, its secondary function is to rear children.

It is natural for modern Americans and other Westerners to underestimate the importance of relatives because in an industrial society they do not seem as needed as in less advanced societies. In non-Western cultures the importance of parents, brothers and sisters, uncles and aunts, nieces and nephews, cousins, in-laws, clan and caste members—all people joined together by marriage and the production of children— is a powerful force. The larger family group cooperates to provide a kind of economic insurance for individuals. They face the world together for many purposes—for rituals, mutual protection, and psychological support (just plain visiting). Such social ties are weakening in many parts of the world as Western economic and social ideas take root, but there are many underdeveloped countries where the old ties remain strong.

Common territory is the base of the second kind of social institution. This means that people sharing the same area, and also having some cultural ties, cooperate to a certain extent.

Such kinds of organizations are primitive hunting bands, village communities, neighborhoods in modern cities, the cities themselves in modern states, and ultimately nations. There can be more coercion than cooperation in some of the largest units, particularly modern nations in the underdeveloped world, but politically they constitute individual units.

In many countries of Asia and Africa there are good-sized tribal groups who do not necessarily want to be part of the nation they are in, and whose cultures are quite different from that of the governing majority; nevertheless, due to military and political control, their economy, their communication with the outside world, and their law systems are in the hands of the central government. In general, such territorial units have grown stronger in the world at the expense of kinship units. The development of the city and state was perhaps the crucial step in this transference of power and authority. Where state control is weak or non-existent, people often settle disputes through their relationship groups; but these matters are settled by the state when it becomes strong.

In Somalia, a country of nomads, where the central government is still weak, murders are usually settled through blood payments or feuds; the lineage (an extended relationship group) takes the responsibility.[8] This is a customary manner of settling such affairs in areas where state police control is not strong; once the state assumes control through its police officials—as in the countries of India and Pakistan— it will not permit a matter as serious as murder to be handled by kinship groups. The ties of kinship may still be strong enough to thwart the state's efforts to bring justice, but it will nevertheless try to prosecute.

The third kind of institution men have devised to organize their relationship with others is the *special interest group or association.* The individuals of such a group may be unrelated and have no territory in common, but they do have some special mutual interest—ritualistic, occupational, recreational, or other. All except some of the most primitive peoples have such relationships.

We in the modern West are quite familiar with organizations of this kind, because all of us belong to some: trade unions, professional societies, church groups, bowling clubs, athletic clubs, fraternities, and many others. In an under-developed country a man may belong to a religious group— Muslim, Christian, Hindu, or Buddhist; he may also belong to an occupational group of leather workers or iron workers, he may be a member of a political party, and he may belong to a brotherhood of athletes. Along with territorial interests, such special interest groups have grown in numbers and importance as state organization has developed.[9] If a man embraces Christianity while his brother staunchly adheres to Hinduism, the traditional family religion, he weakens family relationships thereby. In fact, a Hindu family in India would probably ostracize a Christian member completely. Political party divisions can cause the same kind of separatism, though perhaps of a less emotional nature.

There are several characteristics of social organization that are of vital importance to the overseas American. One is the matter of *rank* or *class difference*. Few peoples of the world assume that all men are equal, potentially or in actuality; the American will have to work within a framework of human differences that is foreign to him. There are traditional systems of ranking individuals and groups; they are based on ethnic, cultural, linguistic and educational differences, as well as upon occupational distinctions and those of economic position.

Sometimes traditional groups are fairly rigid, such as the castes of India; sometimes the distinctions are more fluid, such as those separating people of Spanish and Indian ancestry in Latin America. Almost everywhere there is a distinction between the elite, who have political and economic control of the country, and the relatively underprivileged peasant groups. The overseas American will have to learn the particular distinctions of the country where he is working; he will be compelled to accept the local definition of differences to some extent if he wishes his projects to succeed. It may be possible to gradually introduce some democratic procedures into these countries, but the individual worker will probably be wasting his time and ensuring the failure of his program if he demands an immediate acceptance of democratic methods.

The need to know the class or caste differences in a culture is tied in very closely with the need to know the *power structure;* that is, who controls the village people in fact rather than in theory. This may not be the governmental representative. The local priests or monks may receive more respect and may serve better as leaders. There may be factions in the villages that will cooperate with other factions only under great duress. If this is so, the technician should understand which factions are most powerful and either work through them or at least see to it that he does not unknowingly associate himself with the wrong faction. Many well-intentioned projects have gone astray simply because technicians selected the wrong faction or did not even realize that factions existed.

In the Viru Valley of Peru a project of introducing some wells failed completely and was abandoned because the change agents completely ignored the local power structure. The people had requested the wells and the government provided the technicians; the drillers had good intentions, but they failed to consider the local social organization. They worked through a community council which was an artificial creation of the government and which the local people resisted. Also, the drillers put the first (and only) well on the land of a wealthy landholder and they failed to solicit the help of people who had some social control—the clergy and the old men of the community. The villagers lost interest completely and even became hostile, though the project had been planned for their benefit. The drillers quit and left the village in disgust after the one well was in.[10]

Lastly, there is the problem of *cooperation* in a general sense. Many, if not most, village improvement projects have been developed on the basis of using the village as a cooperative unit. There is some difference of thought among social scientists as to whether the peasant village as it exists in the world today really has a basis for cooperation.[11] In many cultures the peasant villagers are highly individualistic; when they do work cooperatively, it is by factions rather than as whole villages. There are, however, no cultures where people do not work together in groups of some sort. Sometimes the significant group is a religious fraternity, Muslim, Hindu, or a saint's cult; sometimes it is a political party, or a federation of depressed peoples (the Scheduled Castes Federation of India), or even an occupational group (the sugar workers of Trinidad).

If groups are to work together cooperatively, they need a motivation of common interest. It may be community-wide, or it may be restricted to a subsection of a community. The very definition of a social group implies mutual assistance of some sort. A village may not be as tightly integrated as an outside innovator assumes; but the very fact that people live clustered together, rather than spread out all over the country-side, indicates that they cooperate in some respects, that they get some advantage from being together—protection, better marketing facilities, or a richer social life. The change agent should not assume, however, that the village is necessarily the most important cooperative unit to work with initially. It is his job to find out which one is.

☐　　**THE SUPERNATURAL**

When it concerns their activities and beliefs, men are rarely content to rely entirely upon such practical knowledge as is basic for everyday affairs. A people using a culture that embraced no other technique than prayer to grow rice would not survive a generation. And yet despite all the practical knowledge obtained through rational observation that a rice farmer may possess, many occurences can still prevent him from reaping a good harvest. The rain may come too late, or it may come early, then stop when his young plants need it most. An insect plague may descend on the growing plants. A disease may attack the plants. The farmer may get sick just at harvest time.

Such events are unpredictable. What does the farmer do? Does he say, "It is *kismet* or fate and can't be helped," then simply try again, doing nothing further about it? No, not if he is a normal human being. He may say it is fate; but insofar as his culture dictates, he will try to remedy the situation as best he can through his beliefs in the supernatural. He will pray, or make ritual offerings to his god or field spirits, or he will perform some magic rite to bring the rains or drive the insects away. The world to him, as to us, is a place where certain happenings are more predictable than others. He is pretty certain that if he plants a seed in moist ground a plant will come up; he is far less certain that the rains will come in sufficient quantity at the right time.

The only difference between the thinking of the peasant farmer and that of the modern American is that a lot more things about the world are predictable to the American. Even for the American there are vast areas of existence that are not predictable, when he turns to his concept of the supernatural for answers. At certain times he, too, will pray for rain. He may pray for such mundane assistance as financial well-being. The great advances in modern medicine have made human sickness a great deal more predictable to the American than to the peasant; nevertheless, when confronted with a grave illness—such as cancer—for which there is no sure cure, the American, too, will pray. Even in connection with such highly scientific efforts as space exploration, modern Americans turn to prayer. On one of the manned space shots, when an astronaut had been successfully launched and completed his orbits, but disappeared unaccountably near the end of the flight for almost an hour, tension mounted to such a point that a television announcer informed the viewers that "some prayers wouldn't be out of place."

What happens after death is equally mysterious to the American as to the Asian, or African, or Latin American. The point is that Westerners do not think in any different way than do the people of less advanced countries; but they tend to rely less on supernatural explanations, due to their greater amount of practical knowledge. It is fashionable to contrast scientific knowledge with what is called nonscientific. If scientific knowledge is considered as that which is based on objective observation of natural events, then all men possess scientific knowledge. In this sense, the first men who learned to utilize fire and to chip stone spear points gained the first scientific knowledge.

Non-Western people may sometimes use incorrect premises when they lack some of the knowledge of modern Western science. If they have never learned the germ theory of disease they can easily attribute illness to "non-rational" causes such as bad air, bad body humors, or fright. If they know nothing of the earth's rotation or the movement of air currents, they can logically interpret the coming of the monsoon rains as an answer to a rainmaking ceremony, such as one performed annually in Laos. In April the earth is dry and parched when the time for rice planting draws near. The coming of the rains is vitally important and there is a ceremony in the culture to ensure this. The ceremony is performed, and within several days, or at the most two or three weeks, the rains do come. One such ceremony that one of the authors witnessed was followed the same day by a downpour. Cause and effect had been proven. The only way to prove that this ceremony had nothing to do with the rains would be to neglect holding it for several years, but this would mean taking a big chance for a people who do not understand meteorology and are vitally dependent on the rains.

On the other hand, if there are obvious results without too much risk, local people will rarely pass them by to remain dependent on supernatural help alone. Since World War II, yaws, a tropical skin disease, has been wiped out in several areas by the simple use of penicillin. Under the U.S. Point Four Program in Colombia and Ecuador, a campaign was instituted in 1950 among the Negro villagers of the coastal areas to cure yaws sufferers. The people had depended on herbal medicines and native curers before and, although such measures had not been very effective, they still had no faith in the new medicine and doctors when they first came. Despite their fears, some submitted to the injections; the effects were so dramatic that within a couple of years the people were convinced that yaws was one disease the medical doctors could cure. The local people continued to treat other ailments with their own medicines, but they had no doubt that the medical doctor's treatment for yaws was superior to anything they had.[12]

In all cultures, people have their own variety of beliefs about the natural environment, the weather, the functions of the human body and its organs, and the capabilities of human beings. They have beliefs concerned with growing crops, making tools, and getting along with other people. They have their own version of the creation of the universe; their own explanations of disease, death, and the afterlife. Some of what they believe may be demonstrably true; some may be false in our eyes, or unprovable. Some of it may strike us as myth or legend, simple religious faith, or mere popular fancy. Some of these beliefs may be firm and difficult to dislodge, rocks of faith upon which the religion and institutions of the people have been built.

Beliefs are a part of the cultural fabric which people have devised to fit their particular adaptation to life, providing a total explanation of their universe. As was indicated in the yaws campaign, some beliefs are not so vital that they cannot be replaced by equally satisfactory beliefs; but merely refuting them with our own kind of logic is not enough. The most vital fact about beliefs, as far as the technician is concerned, is that people act upon them. Whoever wishes to do a good job of working with people of another culture should master their system of beliefs, or at least such parts of it with which his work is concerned.

☐   **VALUES**

Although not always obvious, another form of belief, extremely important in any culture, is a people's *values*. The popular connotation of the English word implies financial worth, which indicates the centralism of economic considerations in American culture. When we say, "What's its value?" we usually want to know what a thing is worth in dollars and cents. In applying the word to other cultures, we use a much broader definition that refers to beliefs of central importance to which an approbation or a moral or sentimental worth is attached. Instances of such value are: piety in the Buddhist countries; firmness and self-discipline, as among Greek peasants;[13] family responsibility among middle- and upper-class East Indians; masculinity among males in Latin America;[14] personal achievement among modern North Americans.

There can be negative aspects to values; they are usually termed interests, or negative interests. A people may fear ghosts or witches and spend a great deal of time trying to counteract their influence, not because they think them morally good but because they fear them. The Navajo Indians have often been described as a people having an inordinate interest in witchcraft or ghosts, an interest that has often affected their entire behavior. Archeologists in Arizona and New Mexico have reported difficulties in getting Navajos to work as laborers on archeological sites because of their fear of the ghosts of the dead people whose remains they might disturb; the Pueblo Indians of the same region had no such fear and would willingly work on any site if the pay were satisfactory.

Everything and anything in human experience can and does come to have an emotional significance. The people of a culture standardize the emotions, pass them on to their children, and invent or elaborate ways of seeking or avoiding the experiences toward which they feel positively or negatively. They then have the same cultural values. Members of a social group force one another to conform to a considerable extent to these values by rewarding those who follow them and imposing penalties on those who ignore them. Values tend to be conservative; that is, cultural changes in values will be resisted longer than those in technology or economics.

A people such as the East Indians in Trinidad have traditionally valued a large kinship unit and the kind of personalized relationships that go with such an institution; but when they became financially able to purchase cars and thereby increased their mobility, such relationships were weakened. It will nevertheless take some time before they will completely abandon their peasant values of intimate kinship relationships in favor of the impersonal contract and commercial relationships possible through their new mobility and increased financial opportunity. In modern India a man who shirks his family responsibilities may get little financial assistance from his family when he needs it or a poor choice of a bride; a modern American who is not willing to push himself individually will not get the best job, will probably not get the most desirable woman as his wife, and will not be given positions of responsibility in the community.

Not all individuals feel the same emotion to the same degree, but all have to conform to some extent. A culture rewards and punishes and, because of the emotional intensity involved, the individual feels he "ought" or "ought not" to behave in the accepted way. This is due both to an element of compulsion by the society and a built-in ideal imparted to the individual in the growing-up process. Thus the emotional reactions of different peoples are determined by their value systems.

All human beings seem to have the same physiological equipment for the common human emotions. They can all love, hate, weep, caress, and storm with anger. Some of their actions will be individualistic, developed through unique personal experiences, but some of their actions will be common to a group. These common actions are the culturally defined emotions. There are even patterns of abnormality. "Crazy" people are not always crazy in the same way. A supposedly common characteristic of Americans who are classified as abnormal is to make faces, to babble and to make the sounds "brrr" or "buh-buh-buh." On the other hand, a common sign of abnormality for many American Indians is to speak the name of a deceased relative; this indicates that the person must be insane, because this action may bring back the feared ghost of the departed.[15] Each culture has shaped and focused the feelings of its people in its own way. In such matters any overall theory of human nature is apt to be unreliable.

The change agent wishing to transfer a new idea to the

people of another culture must have more knowledge than merely a list of customs and "hard facts." He must deal with the world of values. The technical, social, and supernatural customs of another people do not need to stand the test of utility, efficiency, or truth in the American's sense. They may be the objects of so much emotional and moral value that no one wishes or dares to test them. Some such concepts may be matter-of-fact, others ridiculous, and still others sacred or glorious; but they are nevertheless a vital part of the culture and cannot be understood simply on a basis of Western values. The innovation will have to be fitted into the local value system as well as be adapted to the more obvious customs.

A story is told of a scientific visitor who was shunned by local Moroccan Arabs because he had brought along a large supply of clean, bottled water. He did not know that they equated toleration of dirty drinking water with manly rugged- ness; he was consequently considered an effeminate weakling. "An old Arab hand" suggested an alternative that improved the visitor's status. He circulated a rumor that the scientist was a holy member of a religious sect that obliged him to drink ritually pure water. Piety being a highly prized local value, the scientist's masculinity was restored in the eyes of the Arabs.

☐   FUNCTIONAL INTEGRATION

In the previous sections we have treated human behavior and beliefs in separate categories—language, technology, econ- omy, social organization, supernatural beliefs, values—as if they existed in isolation. It is useful to subdivide culture in this way for descriptive purposes, but there are no such sharp divisions in the actual operation of a culture. If a rice farmer is asked what is necessary to ensure a good crop, he will give a description of the techniques of planting plus an indication that if the gods are willing to send sufficient rains at the right time and keep insects out of his fields, then he will be successful. The ritual as well as the planting techniques are both part of the same process to him. We would consider this as two separate processes—one supernatural, the other natural or technical; but such a division would not exist in his mind.

Very often economic activities are intimately interrelated with social customs and religious beliefs. The Zulu tribes of South Africa, like many other African tribes, depend on cattle as their primary source of food. But cattle also have social meanings. To obtain a wife, cattle must be exchanged between families of the bride and groom. This exchange is a guarantee of good faith and good behavior on both sides. Also, at least once a year, Zulus must sacrifice an ox as propitiation for the spirit of the deceased head of the family; the whole kinship group must then feast on it in a special way.

Many other customs[16] could be cited to show how different forms of behavior are, to more or less degree, *functionally integrated* into a culture and tend to reinforce one another in fulfilling the personal needs of the individuals or in maintaining social cohesion. In an old, stable, well-integrated culture, customs show close consistency, congruence, and mutual support. In the case of a few cultures, customs may be functionally integrated to such a high degree that a comparatively simple change can cause a culture's downfall. The introduction of the steel axe among Australian aboriginals caused a dissolution of the prestige of the older men, a loss of the trading partnerships between tribes (which had depended on the exchange of stone axes), and destruction of the tribal myths which had been central in explaining the peoples' place in the universe.[17] Very few cultures are this highly integrated, but all are sufficiently integrated that one cannot expect an introduced change to affect only one single custom or form of behavior.

Even minor customs that to us may seem merely petty manners, such things as idle play and children's games, appear in a new light in this sense. Children's games are often play-actings of adult roles and thus inculcate the values and customs of the culture in a way that formal schooling might neglect. All peoples have developed a series of ceremonies to mark important stages of man's life, such as the Western ceremonies of christenings, confirmations, weddings, and funerals. These are by no means unimportant ceremonies where wealth is uselessly wasted. They are indispensable trial-and-error methods for preserving individual mental health and group stability through the necessary but difficult changes in human lives. Like other customs, they perform the obvious (overt) functions that the people themselves can describe, and also the less obvious (covert) functions of preparing the participants for new roles and allaying the shock of change that might threaten social order and social continuity.

This covert function of customs is not easy to detect but it can be used very constructively. It took shrewd insight into Navajo ways to realize that grandmothers who were camped on the floor of government hospitals beside the beds of pregnant mothers were fulfilling a custom more important than just visiting. They were transmitting child-care lore to the young mother as well as comforting her. By insisting on keeping the grandmother out, a lot of expectant mothers would also have been kept out; and secondarily, a vital means for the transmission of culture would have been destroyed.

A culture in its entirety does not just consist of technological, social, supernatural, and valuational aspects that are interrelated by functions serving individuals and groups in an obvious way; these facets of culture are also linked together in an intricate structure that contains ever-widening and overlapping emotionally-toned interconnections. This is one of the main discoveries of anthropology—that no culture can logically be divided into separate parts and be truly understood. To the technician, the implication of this discovery is great; for each single bit of custom is liable to endless ramifications as it plays its part in contributing to the whole culture.

☐ **CULTURAL FOCUS**

The linkage in a functional manner of both the obvious and obscure aspects of customs makes up the organic whole of a culture. However, in addition to being interrelated, these customs often add up to a principal common interest, or perhaps several of them. Such main interests will determine what most individuals value and seek for themselves, what really motivates them. It may also be the clue to their accepting a technical change.

For the Zulus and other herding peoples of South and East Africa, their cattle occupy the center of their interests. These peoples have elevated cattle from objects of practical use in making a living to objects of prestige, display, and ceremonial concern central to their lives. In the 1940's a failure to get one group of Zulus to cut down their herds was due to an underestimation of the importance of the animals. The Europeans directing the program assumed that the major use of cattle was to produce milk, to serve as draft animals, and to indicate wealth. They knew that the Zulus used the exchange of cattle for obtaining wives; but they thought that money could just as easily, or more easily be used as a means of exchange. The Europeans were willing to compensate the tribesmen for whatever cattle were destroyed. In terms of obtaining more milk and having good draft animals, the Zulus would be better off, since the remaining animals would be much stronger and more productive.

All these assumptions, however, overlooked the deep symbolic value of cattle. The transfer of cattle at a marriage was much more than a cash transaction. It guaranteed good faith, cows serving as pledges in a way in which money had never been considered. In addition, the animals were the center of ceremonial life and were believed to establish an intimate contact with the spirits of ancestors. Moreover, because of the ritualism associated with their cattle, the people had established deep attachments to them. Each animal was named and its individual characteristics were known in detail by the herders. The program was resisted by the tribesmen and, after a long trial period, the innovators had to abandon it.[18]

The attitude of an American farmer or rancher toward his cattle is that they are simply devices for making a profit without too much delay. The cattle have no ceremonial importance nor are they useful in obtaining a wife, except in the indirect way of having a cash value. If raising some other kind of animal—for example, sheep, pigs, horses—should prove more profitable, the American farmer would switch over immediately. His only requirement would be that he thereby better himself economically. The American farmer may have the same basic motivations as a Zulu—to better himself economically, acquire prestige, and even establish good relations with the supernatural—but his cattle are not central in achieving these ends. His cattle provide him profit and thus wealth. With this wealth he can support his church, gain the esteem of his neighbors, and even improve his marital prospects; but he has no deep psychological attachment to his cattle as a consequence. They are merely a basic raw material.

In different cultures the foci of interests and values can be of wide variety. The Hopi Indians of Arizona had a focus on sobriety and communal effort. Individualism was discouraged. Another of their strong interests was in maize (Indian corn), which had much the same importance to them as cattle had among the Zulus. The Burmese have traditionally focused their attention on their religious life, but in an individualistic way; because according to their religion, Buddhism, the fate of each person is in his own hands. Health, the standard of living, and recreation are all affected by religious activities; the Buddhist temple is the focus of village life.[19] The Greeks are reported to stress interests in "Greek-ness," a belief in the glories of the Greek past, and in the individual personality as firm and self-disciplined.[20] Americans focus their attention on "success," individual achievement in both a financial and prestige sense. One should try to be rich; but better than being just rich is to be rich and famous, or at least to be looked up to by one's associates.

Thus, the interconnections of the customs of a people, whether they know it or not, determine their interests and often dictate their individual motives. Ask anyone why he does what he does, and the chain of reasoning that connects his interests begins. Ask an American why he checks with his wife before going out with his friends at night. It is because he respects her as an equal, or wants to consult her wishes, or feels he owes her companionship—all interconnected egalitarian values which make one of the foci of American culture. Ask a Hopi child why he cries when the American school teacher praises him for good work, and we find that it is because he must not stand out above his fellows. His code does not value competition or individual success. This is a part of the focus on the communal village tradition.

It is by searching for such cultural integrations that the focus of interest in the lives of a people is discovered. Adapting a new idea or practice to such a focus is to go far toward winning its success.

3

CULTURAL
CHANGE

☐   **CONSERVATISM**

To many Americans going overseas for the first time it
will seem that remarkably little has changed in some societies
during the past hundreds, or even thousands of years. Men can
be seen working in the fields, employing the same implements
and techniques that were in use at the time of Christ or before.
In Asian villages people can be seen using a potter's wheel of
the same kind that was used in the area four thousand years
ago, or weaving cloth on a loom dating from the same period.
Romanticists describe the villager's life as going on unchanged
generation after generation. It may appear that any ideas of
change are out of place, that these people do not want to
change.

There is an element of truth in observations of the lack of
change in most cultures; there is a definite conservatism present. In each culture there is a built-in drive toward continuity.
In very few cultures will people voluntarily abandon the old
ways to adopt new customs wholesale. The members of each
culture have an ingrained belief that their own ways are
superior to those of others, despite actual achievements. The
technical term for such a point of view is "ethnocentrism,"
which means that a people believes its own group to be of
central importance.

In their proper language, many primitive tribesmen call
themselves "the true human beings," in contrast to other tribes-

men who are regarded as not equally human. Each culture has worked out a system of adaptation to its environment and the necessary mechanisms for giving individuals the psychological satisfaction they require in competition with other cultures in the same area. The individuals have learned a certain technical lore, certain motor habits, and systems of behavior which are predictable to the others; change would upset all this. Change for its own sake is hardly tempting. In the face of the most tremendous odds, any particular culture will attempt to perpetuate as much of its own ways as possible. The American Indian tribes, most of which were politically, economically, and militarily absorbed by white American culture eighty to one hundred years ago, still attempt to maintain what cohesiveness is possible on their reservations.

It is easy for a member of a more developed nation to point out inefficiencies in an underdeveloped nation or to claim that such nations can hardly maintain a superior attitude in the face of their obvious backwardness. However, the seeming unreasonableness of this attitude should not be too hard for an American or European to understand, because he is no different. Man's technical progress has shifted from one culture to another in the course of history; no nation has been in the ascendancy for more than a limited length of time, after which it has been eclipsed by a more powerful nation. In nearly every instance, the technical knowledge of the earlier civilization passed on to the ascendant power.

Writing systems provide a good example of this process. The earliest writing system known was that of the hieroglyphics of ancient Egypt during its zenith. Semitic people adopted the idea and devised the first alphabet during the period of Egypt's decline. The Semites passed the system on to the Greeks, as well as to many other peoples. The Greeks refined it again, used it, and passed it on to the Romans. Before their civilization fell, the Romans passed the idea on to the North Europeans. Ultimately the North Europeans developed a scientific system of language study based on the alphabet idea. No major technical idea was lost in the whole process, although culture after culture was eclipsed and despite each nation's attempt to maintain its own cultural identity. Neither the ancient Egyptians, Greeks or Romans willingly let their cultural patterns pass away.

The same situation still holds with the developed nations. The nations of Western Europe were in their ascendancy during the colonial period, when they made great contributions to the world's technical knowledge. Since the two world wars and the loss of most colonial possessions, their relative power and ability to contribute to the world's technical advancement has decreased. However, they have not accepted this situation apathetically, knowing that man's technical advancement will continue whether they are the leaders, or whether a new world power now holds that position. Each nation attempts to retain what cultural ascendancy it can. Much of the present competition between the United States and Russia stems from the same ethnocentrism; each wishes to be ascendant, neither is willing to accept man's technological progress apart from its own achievements.

The underdeveloped nations are no different in this respect. Each wishes to see its own culture perpetuated. In fact, the drive for technical and economic change itself is viewed by them mainly as a device by which they may survive in a competitive world and yet preserve their own way of life.

☐ **CHANGE IS CONSTANT**

Despite the conservative tendency of culture, resulting in efforts to perpetuate itself, change is constant. The view that life is as it was hundreds or thousands of years ago anywhere in the world is based on superficial observations. In a village in India, one may still see an oxcart similar to that used during the time of Christ, and maybe a potter's wheel and a loom of as old a type; but not far from the village there will be a railroad track or a paved road where the villagers can board a train or bus and go to the nearest town or city. They may use vessels made on the local wheel, but they will also use aluminum pots and pans made in Indian factories. A large share of their clothing will come from factories, either Indian-made or from industrial countries abroad.

Change is constant for the simple reason that people of different cultures are always in competition with one another. During the whole of man's history, people of a culture that has developed techniques superior to those of their neighbors ultimately absorbed or conquered those neighbors. The new techniques may have been only of a military, economic, or political nature; but they were nevertheless sufficient to overthrow peoples of weaker cultures.

We know that the American Indian cultures were destroyed by incoming Europeans who had a superior technology and superior organizational ability. European culture had been changing rapidly during the previous two hundred years; American Indians did not have time to bring about the changes necessary to make them competitive before they were overrun. The cultures that had been developed by American Indians at the time when the Europeans arrived had displaced other, less rapidly changing cultures. The Inca empire of Peru and the Aztec confederacy of Mexico had achieved their preeminence only a short time before the arrival of the Europeans. In both cases, these empires had been built by a local tribe that had developed the organizational ability to expand and absorb all the tribes around it. In these two instances, the superior technique had been in political and military organization.

This competition between peoples of different cultures is the basis of the drive toward modernization by the underdeveloped countries. In the first place, they have nearly all achieved independence from their colonial rulers through political and military harassment (passive resistance, noncooperation, guerilla fighting), techniques which were new, at least to the colonial powers. After receiving independence, these underdeveloped countries soon realized that their competitive position in the world was really quite poor, and that the one way it could be bettered would be through industrialization and modernization of their own techniques. Individuals of these countries may phrase it as trying to achieve a better standard of living; but it is really an attempt to perpetuate their own cultures through technical and economic changes.

There are two forces in culture, seemingly contradictory, but not necessarily so. The first is a people's attempts to perpetuate their culture to preserve its traditional customs. This causes *conservatism*, which is reflected in the average man who acts as the carrier of tradition. On the other hand, a culture must be made competitive with other cultures, and must be changed as they change in order to ensure its continuity. This leaves a role open for the change agent, the *innovator*. Thus, continuity comes about through change.

☐ CULTURAL BORROWING

There is only one way to achieve something absolutely new in human culture and that is by invention. Invention can take place in any culture, though obviously a new idea can only be built on the ideas already in existence. No one would expect a primitive tribal group to invent an airplane which can fly, though an individual in it might invent an improvement on a bow and arrow or a better kind of paddle to propel canoes.

Although we give a great deal of attention to inventions and inventors, the great bulk of growth in any one culture is fostered by the borrowing of ideas from other cultures. This means that although a new technique, device, or idea must be invented or discovered by some person or group of persons in one culture, it will really only become culturally significant if it is accepted widely within the culture and eventually passed on to other cultures. The principles of modern genetics were discovered in the middle of the 19th century by an Austrian monk, Gregor Mendel. But the science itself did not develop at that time because Mendel's ideas were not accepted. It was not until the early part of the 20th century, when the same principles were rediscovered and widely accepted, that the science of genetics became a cultural reality.

Cultural borrowing is primarily a matter of economy of effort. It is much easier to take over the idea or discovery of someone else, whether it is a neighbor in one's own culture or someone from another culture, than to invent something new. In any culture, individuals are limited by background and time; and the amount of time they can spend on inventing new ideas is limited. They can get new ideas with far less effort by borrowing them; and chances are that the person they borrowed them from had already borrowed them from someone else.

The chief means, then, for bringing about cultural change is the borrowing of ideas by people of one culture from those of other cultures. The occasions for such borrowing are many. Exposure to new peoples and new ideas occurs in conquests, wars and military occupations, through trade, missionary activity, immigration, improved means of transportation, and any other method by which diverse peoples learn the ways of others. Whenever different peoples are brought together they tend to adopt each other's ideas. This process has been so constant in man's history that it is possible to trace the growth of a culture primarily in terms of what has been borrowed from other cultures.

Most cultural borrowing that has occured has not been directed; that is, ideas or techniques have passed from one people to another without any over-all deliberate plan. A trader or missionary may have visited a country with something new, say a new domesticated plant, shown someone how to grow and use it, then taken no further interest in it. If it proved useful, the plant would then be passed from neighbor to neighbor, village to village, tribe to tribe, across continents and seas until ultimately it could be found in the remotest corners of the world.

Some of the most spectacular examples of the transfer of ideas and techniques concern plants originally domesticated by the American Indians, particularly tobacco, potatoes, and corn. Within three hundred years, the techniques of producing and consuming the products of these plants spread around the world. There is hardly any place in the world today where these plants will grow well that they are not grown, no matter how remote the area. Indeed, the history of these plants alone dramatically indicates the willingness of people of all cultures to accept change if the change is clearly beneficial.

In some cultures people borrow more freely than in others. In certain cultures, people may be isolated and not have much opportunity to learn of new ideas. They may acquire some very obvious innovations, such as domestication of the plants just mentioned; but because they are not in the main cross-currents of trade and population shifts, they may never learn of some less obvious changes from which they might eventually derive more benefit than from innovations such as the plants.

A good example of such a benefit is a system of writing. From India, an alphabet was carried eastward, mainly by Buddhist and Hindu missionaries, to various countries of Southeast Asia—Burma, Thailand, Laos, and Cambodia—where it was altered to fit the local languages. But it was the lowland people who were in contact with the Indians. The people of the hills in these same countries had practically no direct contact with them and never learned to write their languages; they also missed many other new ideas which the lowland people learned from the Indians.

Even if a people are in a good geographical position to borrow culturally from others, they may show a reluctance to do so. The values around the old customs may be so strong that people are afraid that new ideas may displace or modify them. Some people show no avidity for the new, just because it is new; others show a long and determined resistance to novelties, a defense against the encroaching outside world. The Japanese decided at one time to close themselves off from the West, but reversed themselves when they realized that they would probably lose out in the long run. They then made an active effort to send out their own people to learn the new technology wholesale, a pattern which the Turks also followed. For three centuries several Southwestern Indian groups have steadfastly rejected new ideas, particularly those which threatened their religious beliefs and communal way of life.

It is a part of ethnocentrism that cultures of greater success and prestige nearly always regard cultural borrowing as a one-way process from themselves to the "lesser breed," the underdeveloped peoples. They are apt to think of such diffusion as the "spread of civilization." And though this is true for most borrowing, the process usually runs both ways, no matter how great the difference between the cultures of the two people. The whole world's history shows that conquerors take over the ways of the conquered, and that colonizers and civilizers learn from their pupils. In the history of China before the period of Western influences, nomadic invaders came from the steppes of Central Asia time after time, only to ultimately become completely absorbed by the people they conquered. The Pilgrims would have starved if they had not learned of Indian corn, fish fertilizing, beans and squash from the Indians. The Normans of England learned much from the lowly Saxons, as did the Portuguese and Spaniards from the Indians and Negroes they enslaved.

When change is not forced upon a people, and when they have a comparatively free choice, they are much more apt to borrow ideas of a technological nature than those of social organization or of supernatural belief. The kinds of things that have been universally borrowed are all of a technical nature. In any culture, the usefulness of domesticated plants, such as corn, tobacco and wheat, or of animals, such as cattle, pigs, and chickens, can immediately be recognized. An even more recent example is motorized transport on land, sea, and air. A man who has been paddling a canoe can easily be convinced that an outboard engine is superior, or that during the rainy season an airplane is the best vehicle to get over areas with almost impassable roads.

On the other hand, ideas of democracy have been carried to many parts of the world and many nations have also heard of American customs of courtship and family relationships; but these same nations have by no means accepted such American ideas and customs as wholeheartedly as they have welcomed outboard motors and airplanes. Firearms and religious beliefs provide another example. Although firearms and Christianity became available to most underdeveloped people at the same time, firearms stayed everywhere, replacing earlier weapons, but Christianity failed to become more than a minority religion in most of Asia and Africa. Christianity did become the predominant religion of Latin America, but the Indian groups there really had little choice in the matter.

People do not borrow indiscriminately; they borrow what will best fit the pattern of their own culture and they favor technological changes over social and religious changes. Once a particular new idea or technique is borrowed, it is reworked and reinterpreted so that it may be integrated into the total pattern. A good example of reinterpretation is the use of plastic cloth, manufactured to serve as tablecloths or drapes, that tribesmen in Laos obtained through trade. Their homes did not require tablecloths or drapes; nevertheless, the tribesmen still had a use for plastic—as raincoats.

Another example, this time as an economic function, was the institution of taxicab ownership and operation on the island of Trinidad in the Caribbean. The same pattern probably holds in many Asian cities. To a taxicab driver in the United States, his vehicle is a means of livelihood, no more, no less; but to the Trinidadian, it is also his personal vehicle and only secondarily a means of profit. The competition is so fierce that he can make only a little profit, yet he can make enough to enable him to pay for a new vehicle every few years and enough for operation and maintenance costs. For his ordinary living expenses he has another job. The taxi in Trinidad has influenced rural life a great deal. It has replaced the traditional bullock cart; but, more importantly, it has created new needs that are affecting the whole pattern of the culture. The village has lost its importance as a social unit, due to the increasing ease of travel; and the auto has become a symbol of prestige, which the bullock cart was not. The auto is often given as a part of the dowry, and young men claim they can get a better-looking wife if they have a good car.

By undergoing modifications, borrowings from another culture effect further cultural changes as they become absorbed into the new way of life. This is a consequence of the functional interconnections between one set of customs and another. The new must be worked into the cultural whole. The same process will occur wth any innovation brought into the culture of an underdeveloped country.

Cultural borrowing is a healthy phenomenon. Those cultures that borrow freely are those that are most viable. There is no better proof for this than the United States, which has taken techniques from cultures all over the world, from the highest to the lowest, in order to develop the cultural whole which has enabled it to assume a position of world leadership. The results have been dramatically described in a famous passage by Dr. Ralph Linton:

"Our solid American citizen awakens in a bed built on a pattern which originated in the Near East but which was modified in Northern Europe before it was transmitted to America. He throws back covers made from cotton, domesticated in India, or linen, domesticated in the Near East, or silk, the use of which was discovered in China. All of these materials have been spun and woven by processes invented in the Near East. He slips into his moccasins, invented by the Indians of the Eastern woodlands, and goes to the bathroom, whose fixtures are a mixture of European and American inventions, both of recent date. He takes off his pajamas, a garment invented in India, and washes with soap invented by the ancient Gauls. He then shaves, a masochistic rite which seems to have been derived from either Sumer or Ancient Egypt.

"Returning to the bedroom, he removes his clothes from a chair of southern European type and proceeds to dress. He puts on garments whose form originally derived from the skin clothing of the nomads of the Asiatic steppes, puts on shoes made from skins tanned in a process invented in ancient Egypt and cut to a pattern derived from the classical civilizations of the Mediterranean, and ties around his neck a strip of bright-colored cloth which is a vestigial survival of the shoulder shawls worn by the seventeenth century Croatians. Before going out for breakfast he glances through the window made of glass invented in Egypt, and if it is raining puts on overshoes made of rubber discovered by the Central American Indians and takes an umbrella, invented in southeastern Asia.

Upon his head he puts a hat made of felt, a material invented in the Asiatic steppes."[21]

Because of its tremendous debt to other cultures of the world, it is only fitting that now, at the peak of its affluence, the United States should make cultural loans to those from whom it received such loans in earlier days. It is like a very successful business corporation returning interest, many times compounded, to those who were instrumental in getting it started. Although in a shorter time span, the underdeveloped countries are now attempting to utilize the same process that the United States used in its period of growth—that of borrowing the best from wherever they can get it for the development of their own cultures.

To here

4

PLANNED
CHANGE

A MAIN PROBLEM

Although unplanned change, through invention and cultural borrowing, has taken place since the inception of man's cultures, the world is now involved in a relatively new process —*deliberate, planned change*. There has been planned change before, but it has ordinarily occurred within a nation or through involuntary participation. Colonizing powers usually attempted to make some changes in the lives of their subjects, but this was done with only a minimum of voluntary participation. In any event the situation today, in which new techniques are brought into a country only when requested by that country, is quite a different matter. This does not mean that everyone in the country wants those changes, but that at least the ruling elite does.

In a sense, this is one of the main problems. When a change that is to be applied to the common man, usually a village peasant, has been agreed upon by a member of the ruling elite and the overseas specialist, the problem is how to convince this common man to accept the new ideas without using force. Another distinct difference between the idea of modern, planned change and unplanned cultural borrowing is the speed with which it is expected to take place. The underdeveloped countries want dramatic changes to occur in a few years, not in centuries. Moreover, the present process of change is worldwide in scope.

The obstacles to scientific solutions in the underdeveloped nations may well be partly economic and financial. These two aspects of development get plenty of attention from both the donor and recipient governments; but most of the difficulties arising from the transfer of techniques and ideas will not be cured by money. Such difficulties stem from the nature of culture and the cultural contact of the peoples concerned, the innovators and the recipients. In a program aimed at local and national collaboration, the interest, motivation, and receptivity of the people to be helped are as important as new techniques and favorable factors of finance, capital, and cost.

Failure of an innovation to take hold may come from a variety of "causes." If local farmers abandon a promising new hybrid corn of great yield because it picks up an unexpected local blight, the "cause" of the failure stems from the inability of the technician to apply his agricultural knowledge well enough in terms of the environment. If the farmers cannot afford the blight-resisting seed bins because the materials are beyond their pocketbooks, the failure has an economic "cause." If the farmers then abandon the new corn because their wives do not like it for the tortillas that make up their diet, the "cause" is due to their food habits, an integral part of their culture.

What spells success or failure in the rapid introduction of new techniques or ideas? This is the basic question for the innovator. There are no set rules that can give pat answers; but there is now a considerable body of helpful information that has been gathered by social scientists and development specialists.

The cultural factors which influence the acceptance or rejection of a new idea can be considered either as obstacles or as stimulants, according to the attitude of the change agent. For instance, a people's beliefs about the supernatural may set certain limitations. If they believe animal life is sacred, a project of setting up an elaborate system of slaughterhouses and meat-processing plants is not likely to be very successful. On the other hand, religious beliefs and institutions may provide the innovator with the means of gaining approval for his

project. A brotherhood of monks may be the most highly respected group in the village; if they back a new idea, it would
be well on its way to acceptance. If people have strong beliefs
which interfere with technical change, positive sanctions may
be found in their sacred literature. As with religious beliefs,
other aspects of culture can either be positive or negative
in their effect. We will consider them together.

☐   **AWARENESS OF NEEDS**

When a change agent arrives in an assigned area of work
and makes a survey of the conditions there, he will almost
always be able to draw up a long list of situations which, from
his point of view, need to be improved. If he is in the field of
public health, many deficiencies will be immediately apparent.
There may be no adequate garbage disposal system in the
villages. Piles of trash may be lying in village lanes just outside
the houses. There may be no system of drainage for waste
water, which will be thrown near the houses, leaving muddy
holes. There may be no adequate drainage system for the
villages in general, with the resultant threat of large areas
going under water in the rainy season. The local wells may not
be properly maintained, particularly on their perimeters, which
may be full of mudholes, places where ducks and water buffalo
wallow. Many people will appear to have malaria and mosquitoes will be numerous. The villagers may go to the bushes
just outside the villages to defecate. The people may drink
unboiled water from any available source, such as polluted
wells, nearby rivers, and even stagnant water holes.

A list such as the preceding one of the conditions present
in most villages in the underdeveloped countries could be made
much longer. If a specialist is concerned with animal husbandry, he could make a similar list. The animals may be
poorly fed. The villagers may not raise proper forage crops
for the cattle nor give any special food to the fowl or pigs,
expecting these animals to pick up whatever scraps they can
find lying in the garbage piles. The chickens may be subject

to many diseases. Practically every year, just before the rains begin, an epidemic may wipe out two-thirds of the flocks. The pigs may be susceptible to the same kind of epidemic diseases. Many of the cattle may contract rinderpest or hemorrhagic septicemia. There are apt to be too many animals, particularly cattle, causing overgrazing and soil erosion. Animals of all types are probably of low quality because there is little selective breeding. Et ceteras could be added to this list, filling many pages and being taken from practically any village where innovators are being sent to work.

The first reaction of a change agent will probably be to begin with what he considers the worst problems. The public health specialist may decide that the gravest problem is that of providing unpolluted drinking water. The animal husbandry expert may decide that the villagers had better start to upgrade the animals by bringing in new breeds and by beginning to eliminate many of the low grade cattle so that there will be more food for those remaining, and so that overgrazing and consequent soil erosion can be halted. If he has the proper governmental authority, he may get started on his projects and seemingly make some headway. The likelihood is, however, that he will eventually find that the local people are either not interested or are only cooperating on the surface, but doing nothing when he or his agents are not present. What has gone wrong?

When the innovator began his work, it was obvious to him that the local people needed help. Even in a general way, they knew they needed improvements. However, their conception of what was needed and his were not the same. He had defined their needs, based on his own knowledge, and though other Westerners would probably agree that these needs were genuine, the local people, who had quite a different base of knowledge, could not see some or most of these needs as genuine. To them, there was no awareness of such needs.

The health specialist, who had decided that the problem of providing unpolluted drinking water was vital, had tried to start a program of purifying the wells and cleaning up around them. He had also started a program to stop the people from getting water from the local water holes and to have them boil their drinking water. However, according to their beliefs of disease, water could not be polluted, at least to the extent of causing illness, so they did not really feel any need to go to this extra trouble. In the case of the animal husbandry situation, the local people might have been quite happy to see the handsome new breeds that the animal husbandry adviser introduced; but they were really not interested in cutting down their herds (cattle were sacred and they also had an important social function in the group), and soil erosion was too remote a problem for them to bother about. They therefore did not feel any immediate need to take care of these problems.

It seems like a pretty difficult situation. The specialist knows what the people need, but they do not feel the same needs. There is a way around it, however. When he comes into the village and the villagers agree with everything he says, the innovator must remember that this is primarily because of his prestige as a powerful outsider and not because they are convinced of what he says. He has to win their confidence if he expects cooperation. The only way he can do this is to begin work on needs which they feel. He must make priorities on his list and begin with something that will provide spectacular results. He may find that of all of the items he listed, the particular one that bothers the villagers greatly is the lack of village drainage; for they really dread the time when their houses will be under water. This means that they are aware of the need to do something about this. The change agent can start right here by laying out a plan of simple drainage. Then after the rainy season, which the villagers will spend dry and secure due to the success of his innovation, they may be willing to try something less obvious, for they will now have more confidence in his abilities.

In the case of the animal husbandry situation, the specialist could perhaps try to inoculate the animals just before the epidemic season. There is no doubt that the village people want their animals to live. When the inoculated cattle, pigs, and chickens survive the epidemics, while animals from neighboring villages that have not been inoculated die, the innovator will be in a much better position to begin other projects, those that will not produce such dramatic results, but will benefit the villagers just as much in the long run.

A good illustration of such an approach occurred in a village improvement project in North India. An epidemic of hemorrhagic septicemia broke out in 1949 in the region of Etawah. Before it reached the area, 4,727 cattle were inoculated by the village development planners. Not one of the inoculated animals died, although there were a number of seizures among the cattle which had not been inoculated. The following year about 20,000 animals were voluntarily brought in for inoculation and other plans for improving animal husbandry were then begun.[22]

Over and over again Western-inspired projects have been unsuccessful because of a failure to deal with needs of which the local people were aware. In many parts of the world, public health advisers report that local people can be taught to build and maintain new outhouses, in order to show their progressiveness or to please insistent health officials; but they cannot be brought to use them. With the open bush around, or where village custom decrees that a covering fringe of vegetation be left for common use, why should they? We know that people in Burma first felt the need for provisions of public sanitation when villages grew into cities, and land speculation and opportunities to sell firewood divided up such common property and the fringes of trees were cut down.

Local village people may not be aware that Western science can do something about the disabilities and discomforts of poverty, low crop yield, bad water or food supply, and attendant diseases with high mortality, malnutrition and debility. They may think that most of their burdens are inevitable and ordinary; and their culture gives them a philosophy which, at least in part, reconciles or consoles them.

Once the change agent has helped a village by eliminating flood conditions, or by saving livestock from seasonal epidemics, he must return to the basic problems he originally listed; for, from a Western point of view, he will still have to cope with many important needs of which the villagers are not aware. The people are still drinking polluted water and over-grazing their land with too many poor grade cattle; and they feel no need to change their ways. To be truly effective, the innovator will have to convince them of the need to improve certain situations. This will be done most efficiently in a gradual way, educating them and leading them from one project to the next.

Following his first success, the change agent might tackle the general problem of drainage, since the people have learned the advantage of not having their houses under water in the rainy season. He might begin by trying to get drainage pits dug outside the houses and on the perimeters of the wells, relating this to their comfort and desire for cleanliness. The animal husbandryman might try to work out a system for feeding chickens and pigs, since these animals do not aggravate the overgrazing problem and the villagers will be able to recognize the benefit of maintaining them properly, an attitude which can later be utilized in improving the cattle and reducing their numbers.

In sum, needs of which the people are already aware, should be utilized in introducing change at first. An awareness of needs which may be stimulated by the innovator should be brought about gradually, after he has gained some measure of confidence.

☐   LOCAL ENVIRONMENT

The American innovator usually brings a highly specialized body of knowledge with him, one which has been well tested in his own environment. Although both culturally and physically he will realize that he is in a different environment in the underdeveloped country where he is assigned, he may well not give this realization as much consideration as he should. Many projects have failed simply because a change agent did not concern himself enough with this problem. The complication arising from such failures is that the innovator involved loses the confidence of the people he is trying to assist. If the project is openly experimental and local participation is not being used, nothing important will be lost. However, if the change agent is introducing a technique into the social group without having tested it already, and the local participants are judging his ability on the basis of it, then failure can result in an important loss of confidence on their part.

A clear-cut example of a failure of this sort occurred on the Papago Indian Reservation of Arizona between 1939 and 1949. A system of impounding rain water in a low place or pocket (*bolsa*) and then dust mulching it so it would not lose much moisture through evaporation was being successfully used in Sonora, Mexico. A Civilian Conservation Corps (CCC) well driller on the Papago Reservation heard about it, and transmitted the information to the superintendent of the reservation. After inspecting the system as operated in Mexico, it was decided to introduce it to the Papago. The driller and superintendent worked hard on the project and developed a fair amount of enthusiasm among the Indians. A number of the *bolsas* were constructed and for the first few years good crops were obtained. But then the bad years came one after another. The Indians progressively abandoned the project until 1949, when the last loyal follower planted his last crop.

A number of mistakes had been made in the manner of obtaining the participation of the Indians and in the actual construction of the fields. But the main failure was the fact that the climatic conditions of Sonora, Mexico, several hundred miles further south and several hundred feet lower in altitude, were not the same as those on the Papago Reservation. The frosts and rains came at the wrong time for getting a good crop on the reservation. Also, there was less rain. Some adjustments might have been possible, such as a change in the type of crops, but they were never suggested. The innovators kept trying to do as was done in the Sonora fields. Thus, the whole idea was abandoned after ten years of experimentation.[23] The point is that the environmental problem should have been settled by the innovators before seeking the participation of the Indians. They could have tried one or two small *bolsas* for two or three years before encouraging the

Indians to build them, or at least they could have limited expansion.

One of the costliest of such failures was that of the Kongwa experiment in East Africa for growing groundnuts (peanuts) on a large scale. A large amount of capital and 3,210,000 acres of land were used in this scheme for producing fats needed after World War II. It was based on a nine-week survey which did not provide sufficient information on soils, rainfall, or crop yields. A number of factors entered into the final failure, including lack of the necessary machinery and the inability of the local people to learn the use of machines rapidly enough; but the primary "cause" was that there was not enough rain, a fact which had not been learned through the brief survey.[24]

Similar oversights can occur on small village-level projects. In India, water is stored for use in the dry season by digging ponds (tanks) on the edge of the villages to hold water until the rains come again. In the pilot project of Etawah in North India, some effort had been made to dig more ponds and deepen the ones already in existence. Albert Meyer, the project organizer, reports that in one instance he came to a village where the local development officer had done an excellent job in building up the enthusiasm of the people; at the time of inspection, there were about 80 people working on one such pond. Unfortunately, they had already dug about two feet below the clay layer and into the underlying sand. The pond was useless since the clay layer had served as a sealer; any water that came into it after the deepening would flow right on through.[25]

Any kind of technical project can run into unforeseen difficulties. It happens despite the best of advice in construction projects in the United States. Foundations for heavy buildings are dug in what is surveyed as solid ground but which turns out to be muck or sand. The American engineering firm then makes adjustments in its construction plans, perhaps sinking wood piles into the muck, and the project goes on with little lost, but at extra cost. In a technical aid project overseas the difference is that one is not only working on a technical problem but also trying to influence the minds of men. They have not as yet accepted outside techniques and a failure, due to lack of understanding by the technician, can cause a tremendous loss of confidence.

To generalize, the change agent should try to understand the local environmental conditions as well as possible and if he is experimenting he should not use local participation.

☐ **COMPLEXITY OF INNOVATIONS**

Coming from a culture that has the most complex technology man has ever developed, the Western innovator must work in cultures having relatively simple, unspecialized technologies. He must literally step backward in time in order to deal realistically with the villagers of the underdeveloped countries and the poorer classes of the cities. If it were simply a matter of moving large amounts of money, machines, and technicians into a country, there would be no problem of this sort. But in order to be truly integrated, the new techniques must be adopted by the local people as their own.

When the developers expect and hope to have their new ideas take hold in five or ten years, they should realize that they have set themselves an extremely short timetable. The Western nations grew into their present complexity and specialization over a period of more than three hundred years, each generation building on that of the previous one. The young of the West assimilate a considerable body of technical knowledge even if they do not become specialists in those fields. The young of the underdeveloped nations have far less such opportunities.

This does not mean they cannot learn. The speed with which the people of the underdeveloped nations have learned to use Western devices has been extremely rapid. Still, it is not reasonable to expect a villager who has no familiarity with complicated mechanical equipment or modern systems of irrigation and conservation to be able to grasp within a year or so the latest Western ways of using these, particularly if he is given no extensive instruction periods. Such people can learn if given a chance, but it is only reasonable to do it in steps rather than attempt to force them to make an immediate jump from a simple village technology to one comparable to that used in the West.

The British groundnuts scheme for East Africa failed largely because the environmental conditions were not well understood by the innovators. A second reason, however, was that the plans called for the use of local tribesmen as operators of the mechanical cultivating equipment. They had had no experience with this kind of equipment and, in fact, were frightened when they first saw it. Ultimately, highly paid European technicians had to be brought in for this purpose, which raised the cost of operations so high that the profits were eaten up.[26] There were many Africans who could have managed this equipment, but not rural tribesmen. In general, the people of the underdeveloped countries who understand Western mechanical equipment are in the cities and towns, because that is where the bulk of the equipment is found.

An American-directed animal husbandry program in Laos ran into a similar problem. The advisers introduced highly bred American hogs into some villages in an effort to upbreed the stock. The animals were handsome compared to the swaybacked native stock and there was no doubt that with proper handling of these imports the local villages would get much more pork for their labor. However, the American hogs failed simply because the Lao were accustomed to the most simple methods of stock handling that man has devised. They let their hogs fend for themselves, wandering around the village and picking up scraps wherever they could. They protected them from wild animals, but gave them nothing to eat regularly. It was a kind of symbiotic relationship rather than a highly specialized animal breeding industry as it is in the West. This offhand treatment spelled failure for the project. The American hogs became undernourished and died; and they had little chance to mate with the local sows because the half-wild village boars were much more aggressive. This particular hog program was abandoned.

A chicken program suffered from the same kind of difficulties. Leghorn and Rhode Island Red roosters were put into village flocks to raise a more productive mixed breed. They, like the hogs, just did not get a diet of high enough quality to breed well or to remain healthy. Epidemic diseases, to which the local chickens were more resistant, wiped out many. Some American chickens survived, but even these got no chance to prove their usefulness. They rarely were able to mate with the local hens because they were no match for the game cocks that served as roosters in the local flocks. The chicken expert tried to get around this difficulty by demanding that a villager get rid of all his local roosters before he would put some American ones in the flock. This worked for one generation. Then the sons of the American roosters and the Lao hens took over. Being half village chicken, they were tougher fighters than their fathers and kept the latter from mating. In this manner, each generation became inferior in size and egg producing ability, but superior in fighting.

The main lesson to be learned from these programs is that the animal husbandry people should have scaled their knowledge down to the local level. They did not realize well enough what a highly specialized activity animal breeding is in the United States and how dependent the American animals are on special conditions such as a high quality diet, medicine, inoculations, and clean cages; they did not see that, for primitive village conditions, these animals were just not suitable. American chickens can be raised in Laos and even half-breeds can be successfully reared. However, some facsimile of the conditions to which they are accustomed has to be produced.

A Vietnamese poultry breeder in South Laos did this quite successfully, but he was a graduate of a Belgian agricultural school and knew the latest developments in aviculture. He crossed Rhode Island Reds with local hens; but he kept his flocks entirely enclosed, the chicken house clean, inoculated his birds, and fed them with a concentrated chicken food which he made from local products. In other words, he maintained them in a manner which an American chicken breeder could have understood. In the vicinity of Bangkok, Thailand, there are commercial poultry farmers who use Leghorns and Rhode Island Reds quite successfully; but they handle them in much the same manner as they would be handled in the United States, not under village conditions.

Does this mean that nothing could have been done to upgrade local chickens in the villages? Not at all. Some intermediate steps could have been taken. The change agent could have concentrated on raising the quality of the local chickens by starting feeding programs and inoculating the birds. He could have tried to introduce some breeds which were not as highly specialized as Leghorns and Rhode Island Reds. The brown Leghorns that used to be in American barnyards or some other variety, either American or from some other country, might have been a possibility. They might not be as productive as White Leghorns or Rhode Island Reds, but they would probably have had better chances for survival under Lao village conditions.

The technician must scale his projects down to meet the ability of the local people and the conditions of their culture. Complex innovations require much more time and instruction than simple ones and their complexity provides more chances of failure.

☐   **INTERRELATEDNESS OF CUSTOMS**

The interrelatedness of customs in a culture adds to the complexity of the innovator's problems. Although each custom or institution in a society may serve several functions, very few cultures are so tightly integrated that no change can be incorporated; but in all cultures there is enough integration that a change will affect more institutions than simply the one at which it is aimed. A simple, tightly integrated culture can be disastrously weakened. Fairly elaborate cultures will also change if the innovation has enough importance.

The growth of industrialism and the movement of peasants to cities causes far more than simple changes in the manner of making a living. The Indian villager belongs to a social unit dominated by caste and kinship; he depends primarily on "face to face" social relations. When such villagers go to an industrial city such as Kanpur, they must not only face an economic situation quite unlike that of their village; but they must also adjust to modifications of their social relations and many other customs. All the workers are of the same low class, a social position in which their caste position counts very little. If a man seeks a job in a factory, the personnel manager cares little if he is a high-caste Brahmin or a low-caste Chamar. He will give both of them the same kind of job and station them next to one another, a situation which would not be usual in the village. Moreover, the man of low caste will have no need to show deference to the man of high caste. A process of equalization will have begun, and the kinship relationships of the village will have weakened. In the village where most people are tied to the land, helping one another's kinsmen is a kind of social insurance. Working for a wage and the whole way of life in a city are individual or immediate family affairs.

The relevance of this concept to introduced change is that rejection of a new idea or technique can occur because it conflicts with some other custom of the group, causing unexpected and undesirable consequences. On the other hand, interrelated functions can sometimes prove advantageous in bringing about changes. Following are some examples of such interrelationships.

In Uganda, the people resisted latrines for fear of evil magic, for they believed they must never let enemies know where they defecated, lest sorcerers use their feces to bewitch them. In Afghanistan, the villagers resisted castration of their bulls, not because they did not know that the animals would grow larger and stronger, but because castration diminished the usefulness of the animals for draft purposes. The fields were tilled by attaching a crude wooden plow to the neck yoke on the oxen and the yoke was held in place by the hump on the bulls' necks. If they were castrated when young, the hump did not develop.[27] A problem like this might have been solved if the total function of the animal in the culture was understood. The innovators might have devised a modified type of yoke for humpless animals. They probably never thought of this problem because bulls are no longer used in the United States for traction purposes.

One of the best examples of the rejection of an innovation because of the interrelations of other customs comes from the Spanish-American farmers in Arizona. Here an extension agent introduced an improved breed of hybrid corn, which produced much more than the previously cultivated local variety. He had good relations with the people, spoke their language, and convinced them to grow the corn voluntarily. They did not have enough good animal food and he thought the new variety would fill this gap. The corn produced as he had predicted and for a few years the local farmers grew it. Then, to the innovator's bewilderment, they abandoned it. On questioning them he learned that the women did not like it because they found it too hard to grind and did not like the taste as well as that of the old variety. It was they who influenced their husbands to give up the new variety, for the primary use of corn had been not as animal food but as human food.[28] A solution might have been possible had the innovator known the complete use of corn by these people. He might then have tried to get a variety that would have fitted both their tastes and the need for animal food, or he might have had them try two varieties, one for human beings and one for animals. A third possibility would have been to encourage them to continue growing the old variety for themselves but to use the new variety for animals.

From Africa comes an example of how health can be harmed when a single European health practice is introduced, but where the total complex of European habits is not adopted. In response to European notions of prenatal care, West African women, who had some education and were financially able to do so, abandoned the field work they had traditionally been doing. However, they failed to borrow the European woman's habits of sport and exercise. The unexpected result of sparing these pregnant women the field labor required by their culture, increased, rather than decreased, their chances of ill health and mortality.

An unexpected consequence of change that was turned to advantage occurred among Greek villagers. An antimalaria spraying campaign had indifferent success until the sprayers realized that Greek peasants, like many other peoples in hot regions, slept outdoors in the summer. The sprayers then ceased to limit their spraying to house interiors, and their campaign won acceptance more because it ridded them of troublesome flies and mosquitoes than because it restored manpower to the farms.

Because customs tend to be interrelated, change can be introduced most efficiently if it is presented in an integrated, over-all approach. If an agricultural technician expects to upgrade cultivation practices, he will soon learn that, unless he attends to related aspects of the culture, a number of blockages will result. If he does not initiate an effort to improve the quality and productivity of the animals, the farmers may see no purpose in growing a larger crop. If he decides that compost pits would be useful for making fertilizer, this could be tied in with public health practices, making the village cleaner by putting all the garbage in the pits. If he needs to give the villagers an incentive for growing cash crops, then the problems of markets and roads becomes important; and well or pond digging may be vital in order to provide more water to irrigate the hoped-for new crops. Once a single project has succeeded, say the introduction of an improved plant, there is a seed of confidence sown among the village people which can be made to grow stronger, making the next innovation easier to introduce.

Changes may be rejected or accepted for unforeseen reasons, which probably result from the interrelatedness of customs. Change programs should ideally be developed through *an integrated, over-all approach* that can both solve the problems of functional interrelatedness and continue to build on confidence already won.

☐   **THE NEW AND THE OLD**

Modernization efforts are by definition in basic conflict with traditional ideas, customs, and techniques. The forces of conservatism are strong because however poor, from the Westerner's point of view, the local standard of life may be, it is a successful adaptation which enables these people to get by. Add to this the ethnocentric attitude built into all cultures, and the result is that the new generally has no attraction just because it is new. The local people may want to have a better way of life, but they fear changing arrangements which they already know and trust. Certain changes have dramatic advantages and these tend to sell themselves.

The treatment of yaws, in which the disease is eliminated simply by injections of penicillin, is a case of this sort. However, where benefits are not so immediately recognizable, the problem is more difficult. In such cases, building the new upon the old is probably the best solution; that is, grafting new ideas upon the values, concepts, and institutions that are already present. By completely discounting the traditional, or by defining it as irrational and superstitious, the innovator merely creates distrust between himself and the local people, making them less willing to try anything new. All peoples are pragmatic enough that, if given the opportunity to observe an advantageous change, they will most likely accept it. However, if an innovation is peremptorily presented to them as being the only possible alternative to what they have previously known, they may very well refuse to study it enough to observe its advantages.

Medicine is one field in which this problem has occurred very often. People everywhere are vitally interested in their health, but never having been thoroughly subjected to Western concepts of medicine, many of them have continued to rely on folk medical practices of their own. Some such practices yield practical benefits; others, from a Western point of view, are useless or sometimes (though rarely) harmful. In terms of the interrelatedness of customs and ideas, some practices are not even medical from our point of view, but supernatural. This is why "witch doctor" was introduced into popular English speech as the definition of a non-Western curer; for he not only doctors, but he also takes care of illnesses caused by witches or supernatural beings.

In Latin America, local peoples recognize a large number of diseases which they believe are caused by "hot" and "cold" body humors; some others are attributed to contagion from bad air or bad odors. What we would consider as magical causes are those caused by "evil eye" or "fright" from seeing a ghost or evil spirit.[29] In village India, there are numerous kinds of curers, including those who practice very ancient traditional systems that depend on traditional herbal medicines and drugs, but there are also several different kinds of magical practitioners, including special snakebite curers who must be possessed by a snake god before they can "suck" out the poison.[30] However irrational such beliefs may appear, it has almost always been found most practical to build Western medical beliefs on top of them; to slowly replace the erroneous ones, but not to begin by refuting them before convincing the local people of the superiority of the new techniques. Dr. Carstairs, a physician who worked in village India, states:

"In the immediate future, it devolves upon those who are introducing western techniques in public health and medicine to study how best they can adapt the roles of the doctor, the pharmacist and the public hygienist to fit into cultural expectations. In the process, they may have to consent to assume the mantle of the priest or magician. This does not mean, of course, that they will themselves subscribe to nonrational beliefs, but simply that they will accept the inevitable fact that their own techniques of healing will be accepted 'irrationally,' as indeed they are for the most part in the West."[31]

The new can also be grafted onto the old in other spheres. In the Marshall Islands of Micronesia, the American administrators found that the best arrangement for law enforcement and judicial bodies was to set up a dual system: one of native courts to be handled by the local hereditary leaders according to their own traditions; and another to control affairs which were new and a result of the American administration, with a new code of laws and a separate judicial body.[32] In this way, the new did not attack the old, but was attached to it. As in the case of medical practices, the new may ultimately replace the old, but only when peoples' beliefs have changed accordingly.

Unless they produce dramatic benefits, the easiest way to have innovations accepted is not to have them present an open conflict with traditional values and customs, but rather to graft onto them. Ultimately, they may replace the traditional beliefs but, for the sake of acceptance, it is best that they do not contradict them openly at the outset.

☐ DEMONSTRATION OF INNOVATIONS

The peoples of the underdeveloped nations are as pragmatic as Westerners. They will need clear-cut evidence that the benefits the technician talks about are truly benefits. They have to see them to believe them. This idea is well known by extension agents who have worked only in the United States. The American farmer was not willing to accept hybrid corn until it was thoroughly proved. In the 1930s when it was first being introduced, there was a great deal of resistance. The farmers would talk about fields they knew, criticizing the plants because the stalks were puny-looking compared to the old non-hybrid varieties and because they were shallowly rooted. Storms would blow the plants down, they said.

A farm extension man, who had gone into overseas work, once told us of his problems during the old days when he was trying to get hybrid corn accepted by Texas farmers. He said, "There was one particular area of fairly well-to-do farmers who just wouldn't listen to me. I talked and talked and no one would try the new seed. Finally I decided that I would have to stick my neck out. I found one farmer who jokingly told me he would plant some of the seed on his farm if I would promise to pay the full difference in profit if the new seed produced less than the old variety. I decided I'd have to do it if I was going to make any headway. The field was in a good spot in the middle of a wide valley, just along a road, and you could see it a long way off. He planted half of it with the old seed and half with the hybrid. Luckily for me there was not much rain that year and the hybrid was a drought-resistant variety. At the end of the summer the patch of hybrid corn was the only bright green spot in the valley. You could see it a mile away. I was in! Not only was the farmer who planted it convinced, but he became my unpaid agent. He invited all his friends to come and look, and would even pick them up in his car. After that, it was no time at all before everyone in the valley was growing hybrid corn."

Such a situation is no different from that encountered in the underdeveloped countries. A clear-cut motive for accepting the innovation must be present—economic gain, greater prestige, emulation of others—but even then they must see that the new idea will work. It has repeatedly been shown that innovations snowballed once the first demonstrations were successful. In the Vicos Project of the Peruvian highlands, the innovators provided the means for cultivating blight-free potatoes by setting up a credit system whereby the local Indians could get the seed, the insecticide, and the other materials they needed; then pay it off with a share of the crop at the end of the season. A small group was willing to try this system the first year and their yields were double. Within two years practically all farmers of the 300 families living in the community had switched over; and within six years the community had become the largest potato producer of the region, selling the surplus on the Lima market.[33]

Another dramatic success based on a good demonstration was a soil erosion control project at the Etawah Pilot Project in North India. The banks along the Sengar River were badly eroded, a situation that had already bothered the villagers enough that they had tried to remedy it themselves by building small dams and plugging gullies. However, their efforts had always been washed away in the rainy season and they had finally given up in discouragement. It took a lot of persuasion to convince any of them to try again, but finally seven

villages in one small watershed agreed to one more try.
Through good extension guidance, the structures built were
solid and did not wash away when the rains came. The villagers could see with their own eyes that the soil was not being
carried away and, to the contrary, was being built up from
the silt washed in by the rains. The first effort reclaimed 140
acres. Later in the same year, another 140 acres were reclaimed, in the following year another 370 acres, the year
after 2,500 acres.[34]

While positive results can bring about a quick change in
the thinking of tribal or village people, negative results can
do much harm, probably far more than with the American
farmer. If the extension agent working in Texas had failed with
his hybrid corn experiment, he would have found it more
difficult to convince another farmer to try again; but this would
concern two men of the same culture. Failure would not have
changed their basic relationship or ability to communicate
with one another. In the case of the Hindus, or the Peruvian
Indians, the entire prestige of Western technology was put at
stake when a demonstration was made. A negative result, such
as the failure of the Leghorn roosters to survive in Lao villages, or the error of the technician in India who dug below
the clay level in trying to deepen village ponds, reinforces
the lack of belief in nontraditional ways that the local people
had before the innovator appeared on the scene. In the same
way that he must understand the environment, the innovator
must also know that what he is doing will succeed.

A convincing demonstration can only take place in the
village or environment where it is to be applied. State agricultural farms or any other kind of controlled environment
may convince the specialists, but the villagers must see the
demonstration on their own territory. They must see practical
changes where no outside justification is called upon. They
may believe that the soil or other factors which they cannot
duplicate are responsible for good results at the agricultural
station; but if the demonstration succeeds on their neighbor's
field, a field they know, grown by a man they know, the evidence will be much more convincing. One excellent method

of introducing new agricultural practices is to draw a lesson directly from experimental science by setting up a control field. If one part is sown with the new seeds or fertilizer and the other part prepared in the traditional way, the contrast can be striking.

Like the corn farmers in Texas, most people in the under-developed areas are pragmatic and demonstrations are necessary. They must, however, be well controlled and have positive results; otherwise, any confidence the change agent may have initially inspired will be completely lost.

□   **PREDICTABILITY OF
THE INNOVATOR'S BEHAVIOR**

It is no easy task for an outsider to get people to change their pattern of doing things. They may be partially convinced that a new idea will be advantageous, either through demonstrations, or because they are impressed by the innovator. He comes to them as a person of high prestige, which in itself will give him influence. However, if his idea or project is to require some period of time before it can be considered truly successful, he is going to have to be continuously predictable. Among peasant villagers and the poorer classes in the cities, the prevalent attitude toward outsiders is usually one of doubt and suspicion. Such misgivings can only be dispelled by continuous positive evidence from the outsider. Loose promises, ill-planned projects which must be abandoned, or unexplained behavior will only harden the incipient mistrust of such villagers, and all initial gains will be lost.

In the 1930's U.S. Indian Service personnel gained valuable experience concerning the need to explain their programs clearly to the people concerned. In order to halt erosion and to improve the quality of the Indians' livestock, a conservation program was undertaken on the Navajo Indian Reservation in the "four-corners" region of the Southwest. The main project was to numerically reduce the animals to the carrying capacity of the range; the technical aspects of the situation were well understood. Some 400,000 sheep and goats, as well as a number of horses, were bought by the government and destroyed, land conservation projects were undertaken by the CCC, sheep-dipping procedures set up, and special grazing rules established.

Erosion of the land was effectively halted; therefore, from a technical point of view, the project was successful. Viewed psychologically, however, the project failed utterly, mainly because the Navajos never really understood what the technicians were trying to accomplish. No one had ever enlightened the Navajos concerning the dangers of range depletion and erosion due to excessive grazing; therefore, to them, the complicated procedures of destroying animals and allotting pasturage were inexplicable. The American administration, which was again changing their way of life, now appeared to them as a completely unpredictable bureaucracy. One Indian was quoted as follows:

"Before, in the six jurisdictions, you could go to your Agent. Now you got to go to Window Rock and you go to every department and never find out anything. I myself went to Window Rock many times to find out different things, and the longer I stayed the less I knew—(they were) just passing the buck. I ask the superintendent—he sends me to office so-and-so. I go there and they send me somewhere else."[35]

In such projects, the cooperation of the people is essential; the recipients' usual reaction will be one of complete lack of interest, if not hostility, if the innovator's behavior is unpredictable.

A conservation program in Chile affords a good example of a positive application of predictability. The program was initiated by an American who offered to build some terraces for local farmers. The American at first explicitly informed them that the work could only be considered experimental until the exact rainfall characteristics of the area were known. When the rainy season came, he spent hours checking the terraces with his Chilean trainees. His project was successful, largely because the local farmers trusted and supported him.

A negative instance of predictability occurred in a Haitian

irrigation project, where the innovators engendered considerable distrust. On one occasion they informed the local peasants that the water would be cut off for several days so that repairs could be made on the irrigation canal. When they changed their plans and left the water running they failed to inform the villagers. Several weeks later they sent out a similar notice; this time, however, the peasants paid no heed and, when the water was cut off, they lost their crops.[36]

Concerning the Etawah Project of North India, one of the main complaints from villagers was that the innovators, here the so-called "village-level-workers," made too many promises that were not fulfilled. Until the situation was absolutely in hand no promises should have been made; then, once made, the village-workers should have considered such promises as obligations of extreme importance.[37]

The innovator must realize that his initial actions will be judged supercritically. If he fails to be predictable or to live up to his promises, the local people will lose all of their confidence in him.

☐ **PARTICIPATION OF RECIPIENTS**

Many failures have occurred because change agents have not taken the trouble to involve the local people thoroughly enough in their projects. Technicians have given too much emphasis to the technical aspect of their jobs and not enough to the human aspect. This has too often resulted in installations of great efficiency built only to be abandoned or never completely accepted by the local people.

The average technician is highly specialized and from his point of view can observe the needs of an area very clearly; he wishes to get something done and tries to explain both the needs and the solution to the local people. Sometimes they do not understand as fast or as well as he wishes; but he is still convinced he knows what they need, so he pushes ahead with the project. Rarely will the villagers openly contradict the foreign adviser, for he is high on the ladder of important men and they are used to authoritarian directives coming down from above. However, if his suggestions are too far out of line, they may not cooperate at all; usually they will at least cooperate on the surface, but they will do nothing further unless they have accepted his ideas on their own.

Villagers and the poorer classes of the developing countries have lived for a long time under authoritarian rule; the government, both colonial and postcolonial, has been a remote agency whose main activities have been to collect taxes and enforce the law. The individual peasant may have seen some national project, such as the construction of a road, bridge, railroad or even a school, and he may even have used some of these; they were still the government's projects, not his. The traditional attitude of the peasant has been to evade the authority of government officials, and, from his point of view, for good reason. Until recently, whenever they appeared, it was usually to collect taxes, to enforce a law which he did not understand, to squeeze some of his hard-earned money from him, or to interfere generally in his life without giving him any recognizable benefit. This relationship is now changing in many parts of the world due to the rise of mercantilism, the growth of middle classes, and increasing efforts to incorporate peasants into the national economy; but in most underdeveloped countries, the peasant's attitude concerning government representatives is, on the whole, unchanged.

The outside expert enters the scene as an official closely associated with the government, as well as a man of high prestige because (from the peasant's point of view) he is a wealthy and well-educated foreigner. If he does nothing positive to involve the local people's participation, they will react to him as they would react to one of their own officials; and, if the project requires cooperation from the people being aided, this can be fatal.

A project is not going to get far unless it satisfies the conscious needs of the people, and the expert's opinion as to what the people need is not enough to win their cooperation. Even if a new idea or technique fills needs of which the local people are already aware, it may fail unless the local people accept it as their own and are actively involved in all stages of the planning. Two well drilling programs in South Laos indicate clearly the failure that can result from high-handed procedures.

The first project was a group of seven wells dug in the town of Paksé in 1956 through the Laotian government's public works department, but with the advice and financial assistance of an American agency. The wells were deep and fairly expensive to construct for most of them had to be drilled by dynamiting through layers of solid rock. They were placed in various neighborhoods in the town where they could serve large groups of people. They were capped with concrete and good pumps put on them.

The people were definitely aware of the need for good water and there was a great demand for wells. Without them, water had to be carried from the Mekong River or be bought from water carriers. Since no one was assigned responsibility for these wells, they were consequently regarded as "government" wells. By 1958 all had broken down. The American regional agricultural advisor repaired them all in that year, but still did not bother about the problem of designating responsibility for them. Before he left the country a year later some had broken down again, and in 1960 all of them were once more out of order.

In 1959, a second project of well installation was undertaken in the province of Champassak of which Paksé was the capital. This time the wells were driven much deeper, under a contract with an American well driller using an expensive rig. The well driller's technique was to consult with the Laotian officials to find out which villages had the greatest need of wells. He would then move in with his paid crew and rig and drill. In all, about fifteen wells were drilled, but five of them were at government installations or at the homes of Laotian officials. In each instance, the villagers were quite happy to get the wells and used them regularly as long as they were operative.

Within a year, however, a good half of the wells drilled in the villages were out of order. Usually the breakdown was of a minor nature that could have been repaired locally either through the public works department or through local machine shops. But the government assumed no responsibility for such repairs, nor was there anyone in the villages who did. The villagers, who considered these wells as belonging to the "government," not only made no effort to have them repaired, but also did not even attempt to keep the well areas in good condition. They pumped water constantly while the pumps worked, allowed the children to play with the handles, and permitted the excess water to fall on the surrounding ground where it created mudholes in which ducks splashed about and water buffalos wallowed. Despite all this, the village recipients were at no time consulted or made to feel that the wells were anything more than "government" installations.

Meanwhile the wells drilled on private land continued to be operated efficiently. Responsibility for them was assumed by the people concerned. The Laotian officials, whose attitude toward the government was different than that of the villagers, knew that if they failed to take the initiative in keeping their wells operating that no one else would. Moreover, they had better access to, and information about, repair facilities.

Quite a number of things could have been done to make the wells work in the villages. Although the villagers were not equipped to undertake the actual drilling of the wells, they could have managed their maintenance and repair, and they should have been consulted about these chores when the project was first started. Some person or institution in the villages should have been given supervisory responsibility— the village school teacher, the village headman, or the Buddhist monks. The Buddhist monks would probably have been best for this job, being the most highly respected individuals in such villages. One of the village wells had by chance been put into a Buddhist temple ground and was the only one which had not only been maintained but also been improved. When a metal part which had been attached to the handle broke, they managed to have it duplicated in very hard wood; and, surprisingly enough, it functioned quite satisfactorily. They had also paved an extensive area surrounding the well with concrete so that excess water would not accumulate.

Everyone in the village was welcome to draw from the temple well.

It might be argued that the villagers would not be interested in communal property, but this is doubtful. They had a long tradition of working on the temple grounds, and of building structures both for the monks and for themselves. Many schoolhouses, as well as some bridges and roads throughout the area, had been built as communal projects. However, from the very beginning, these projects had been their own. To insure the proper maintenance of the wells, it would have been necessary to transfer them psychologically to the villagers.

Fortunately, to offset cases such as the preceding ones, an equal number of instances can be cited where innovators have successfully enlisted the active participation of the local people. One outstanding conservation program took place between 1947 and 1949 on the Papago Indian Reservation, where several thousand acres of land were reclaimed for pasture. The conservationist there had already conceived a plan of action but, before undertaking its execution, he presented it to the district people for their decision. First, through an Indian bus driver who lived in the village, he explained his plan to the local headman. He then let the bus driver and an extension employee, who was also an Indian, do the necessary persuading. When the group agreed to build the earth dikes suggested by the conservationist, he brought in an engineer to survey the area. The Indians objected to the results of the survey, but the conservationist was wise enough to recognize his mistake—he had not consulted them about the survey but had made it on his own.

His next move was to have it redone after consulting with them, and this time they accepted it. The change made was minor but the Indians were again reassured that it was their project. From that point on, he reemphasized his role as that of adviser, not planner. The Indians did the work and when the rains came that fall the dikes held as predicted. The program was intensified the next two years and proved to be quite successful.[38]

The change agent sometimes tends to concentrate his work on the educated or on those who are already fairly well off, for it is easier to deal with people whose culture is not too different from his own. The justification for this tendency is that such groups will accept change more readily. There is undoubtedly less of a problem of communication and participation with such people and the innovator will probably find it more convivial to work with them.

However, even if these upper-class groups accept change, the main problem, to get the peasantry who really need change to accept it, will still be present. There are those who claim that a kind of ripple effect will take place, that knowledge will pass out from the moderately well-off landowners to the poor peasantry. There is probably some truth to this, and yet backward areas and sections of a population can remain backward for a long time while their more favored countrymen move forward rapidly. The Papago, like many other American Indian enclaves in the Southwest and the Spanish-American farmers, have been in contact with Anglo-Americans and have seen what the Anglo-American farmers can do for a hundred years, yet they still lack their efficient techniques. A direct attack on the problem, such as that made on the Papago reservation, brings changes about much more quickly.

Two of the most successful development programs on record are the Vicos Project for Peruvian Indians and the Etawah Pilot Project in rural India. In both cases the full participation of the villagers was enlisted and this direct approach changed the communities dramatically; so dramatically that the project planners were able to leave the regions, their job done, within seven years. From that time on, their mode of living revitalized, the villagers were able to cope with their own problems.[39, 40]

If change is to be fully incorporated into the life of the people, their full participation in planning and undertaking the work itself must be woven into the project plans both from its beginning and throughout all of its stages. There are, of course, projects that can only be handled on a national level such as airports, national highways, and administrative systems. Understandably local participation will be minimal in such instances and it should be made clear that such projects will remain the responsibility of the national government. Those which are planned for the acceptance by and the responsibility of the peasantry, or of a local group, will have to involve their active participation through all stages of planning and implementation.

☐ **SOCIAL STRUCTURE**

A powerful determining factor in any kind of human relationship is the nature of the social groups which control the behavior of the individuals. This has also been found to be a crucial factor in a large number of cases of introduced change. The innovator is faced very early in the planning of his project with the question, "Who shall I work with?"

He usually works most with officials in the civil service of the host country or members of the educated class. This official can be expected to have more or less accepted the specialist even before they start working together, although they may see problems in a somewhat different light. This person already knows something of the expert's specialty and, at the very least, the two of them are in agreement that they are going to try to introduce some kind of change. However, the innovator will still have to face his chief hurdle, namely, to transfer the change to the people of the uneducated classes, usually peasant villagers; the cooperation of their social groups is absolutely indispensable if the change agent is to accomplish his job. There is always an official administrative structure leading down to the village level, the adviser's counterpart being a part of that structure. On the village level, there is usually a headman and sometimes a council of leaders, either designated or confirmed to office by the government.

It is easy to assume that village authority rests with these people. The counterpart will usually tend to act as if the government headman were the real leader, since he is a functioning part of the government. Unfortunately, this may not be the case, for government, to the underprivileged in many parts of the world, has been until recently a group of people best avoided. Appointive officials, even if they are villagers themselves, have also acquired some of the stigma of "government." The villagers will cooperate with such leaders when it is unavoidable but whenever they have a real choice, they will not. In such communities there may be traditional power organizations which the newly independent governments, or their colonial predecessors, have ignored; but this does not mean that these organizations have ceased to influence the local people.

One of the best examples of powerful traditional organizations that have been largely bypassed by modern governments are the established religions—the Catholic Church in Latin America, Islam in Asia and Africa, Hinduism and Buddhism in South and Southeast Asia. With the possible exception of Hinduism, these religions have been usually in great part intertwined with the other traditonal organizations of the villagers; many of their activities have been cooperative endeavors directed by the monks, priests, or mullahs. Schooling has often been in their hands, as has the general welfare of the village. Religious ceremonies, such as the Latin American fiesta, have often been the only important foci of common interest of all members of the community.

Even today, when most national systems of authority in the world are secular, religious organizations have not lost all of their authority in the villages. They have usually remained quite influential; so much so that, if they oppose a change, it has little opportunity of acceptance. A good example of such religious authority was the wells drilled in the Laotian villages, when the only well properly maintained was the one placed by chance on the grounds of a temple. The monks had enough influence and prestige to get the villagers to maintain it, a result that no village headman had been able to obtain.

This does not mean that religious organizations are always the dominant force in the communities of the underdeveloped world. Their power has been sapped, both by the secularization of governments and by the growth of extra-village, middle class influence in many areas.[41] Still, they often have enough force to control opinion. The planners of the Etawah Pilot Project in North India took advantage of this fact in a very sensible way. Though they made no overt effort to work with the priests in their village projects, they did name their fortnightly project newspaper *Mandir Se* (From the Temple). Its masthead showed a Hindu greeting the rising sun in traditional posture, standing beside some Hindu temples.[42] The coverage of the paper was mostly news items and practical advice to villagers, but it probably had a secondary effect of allying the Brahmin priests to the cause of change.

Another type of relationship that may affect acceptance of a new idea or technique is that of kinship. Hospitalization, particularly if it involves isolation, has been resisted by people in many parts of the world because they have felt they needed to be with their kin most during such a crisis as sickness. The hospital has seemed a lonely, sterile place, and also a place where people have often died. The simplest method to get around such fears has invariably been to include the kin group in hospitalization in some manner, even if it disrupts Western ideas of care. Dr. Schweitzer has reported that, even though he used the least amount of discipline possible in his Congo hospital, every possible effort was nevertheless made to avoid going there, mainly due to the separation of the patient from his kinfolk. Lepers would not visit the clinic unless they believed they could get chaulmoogra oil for home use; and patients in the hospital who had dysentery would hide the fact because treatment would curtail their freedom and put them under supervision.[43]

In many areas leprosy has been found to be difficult to treat whenever the doctors insisted on isolating the infected persons from their families. In Iran, a German doctor discovered a system used by the local villagers in which the leprous person did not need to leave his family, but was isolated in one room of the family house. There were separate utensils and the leprous person was required to avoid any intimate contact with the other members of the family, but was still able to talk and visit with them through a window or doorway, thus eliminating the worst hardships of exile and isolation. Since leprosy can be contracted only through long and intimate contact, such measures were sufficient to prevent the spread of the disease. Only with such a system would families report leprous individuals in their midst. The doctor recommended that the Iranians should build their modern medical services on this traditional pattern.[44]

It may prove very difficult to get work done across barriers of caste and class differences. Ordinarily, if a project is to be a cooperative venture, the local group in ascendance will refuse to work on an equal basis with the groups they consider lower. Even when such working together is forced upon them, their culture may have manipulative devices to sidestep the ideas of foreigners. When the American forces took over the administration of Palau in the Pacific, among other changes that they introduced was the institution of free elections. The Palauans had been accustomed to a two-class system of elite and commoners. However, they had long lived under a series of foreign governments—Spanish, German, and Japanese—and had become adaptable. They did not object openly to the elections but, when they were over, the same persons who had held the offices by hereditary right were still in power. Some were removed by the Americans because of certain unacceptable qualities, but most of their replacements were later found to be merely front men, still controlled by the elite in the background. Some changes in power structure did take place but, in general, the traditional two-class hereditary system persisted.[45]

This problem of vested interests is a fairly important one. Change seldom originates with individuals or groups who benefit, or think they benefit, by maintaining the status quo. A touchstone of innovation, indeed, is the identification of those who will benefit. Some cultures possess classes and persons who have a genuine concern for benefits to the community at large, realizing that the good of the individual is largely served through the community. This may not be the case in other cultures. In still other cultures, there may be classes and persons who accept change for themselves, but wish to deny it to those whom they rule or dominate. In this regard, there is little difference between the underdeveloped countries and the developed ones.

A telling example of this problem of vested interests comes from the United States, from an Alabama town which decided to embark on a community health program. They chose the project themselves and carried out the work, which was to be divided in two phases, an inventory of health needs and an implementation program. Members of the local university were called in for consultation. The planners were interested in bettering conditions in the whole community and wanted broad participation.

However, many of the most important goals were never reached and full participation was never achieved because the community was divided in classes and the vested interests were not willing to disrupt the status quo. The organizers were members of "the community," white members of professional status and white-collar workers for the most part, and the joiners of civic organizations. The other two classes, Negroes and white laborers, were not brought into the planning and they consequently showed little interest. The interests of the laborers were different from those of the professional people and they were represented by their own agents, union organizers, who were "outsiders" to the professional people. Managers resisted giving out information on the working conditions in their plants for fear that the union organizers would use it against them. The Negroes were in a position traditionally inferior to that of the whites and "the community" would not let them abandon this role. They kept the right of initiating action and supervised the activities of the Negroes who did work on a health questionnaire which had been devised by the whites. There were never any integrated committee meetings. Resentment was created among those who favored integration.

Although the inventory did manage a few changes in the community, they were of minor importance and principally of benefit to the professional white class. The committees which were organized to help the other classes, the Industrial Health Committee and Rural Health Committee, were abandoned.[46] The town was divided into separate classes, each with varying aims, and the one class which had the most power had a vested interest in not bringing about disruptive changes.

There may be no overt resistance from those with vested interests when it becomes clear that the society they lead must either accept the new to catch up, or else go down in subjugation or dislocation. In the case of the Palauans, the noble clans and families of chiefs did not resist the American system of elections, but nevertheless saved their vested interests to a certain extent by learning to put their sons in the higher posts of the administration as interpreters and aides to American personnel, thus continuing their influence indirectly. Changes will be accepted most easily when they support an established cultural or social order, unless the society is already in the ferment of social change or a new social class is emerging. The innovator must ask himself, "Who wants to make capital for himself from my innovation? In the light of my purpose is he worth supporting?"

Because of vested interests in village life, as elsewhere, factions arise and the competition of individuals and groups is as apparent as are cooperative tendencies. There are always some areas in which there is a base for cooperation, however, and it is up to the innovator to find these if his project depends on mutual action. Even in India, where the villagers are subdivided into fairly rigid caste groups, points of mutual interest can be found.

It is vital that the innovator understand the social groups with whom he must work. If he chooses the wrong person or group for leadership he may fail to get the participation of the majority. Vested interests operate in all cultures and, if their aims can be properly channeled, they can be useful to the innovator. Otherwise he would do better to avoid working with them directly and to keep himself aloof from power factions.

☐ **PRACTICAL BENEFITS**

The success or failure of a change agent's project will ultimately depend on the motivation of individuals; therefore it is worth considering what makes individuals desire an innovation. The basic motivation is undoubtedly the same as that which causes Americans to accept a change—some practical benefit. Since the man in a traditional society is pragmatic and just as concerned with his own self-interest as the man in Western society, he will accept a change offered to him if he is convinced it will improve his life. Many villagers of traditional societies have lived for a long time in circumstances in which it was virtually impossible for the individual to improve himself financially, or in which the difficulties involved in trying something new were so great that it was not worth taking a chance. A peasant working under a landlord who reaped most of the fruits of his labor would have little incentive to increase his output, a situation widely prevalent in Latin America and Asia until recent years. In such a situation, a change in agricultural practices would have helped the individual very little.

The peasant's lack of incentive could also have been brought about by oppressive taxes and other governmental controls. A third type of limitation could have resulted from continued unrest and instability in a country, creating a situation in which the individual could put little faith in the future. In such a case, no one would be likely to try to improve his land and his physical assets, for he would fear losing capital he invested.

It was a widely held belief in Laos that villagers were not interested in growing surpluses of food for self-improvement. This belief seemed supported by facts, at least superficially. Each villager normally grew just a sufficient amount for the needs of his family. In very favored regions a few grew small surpluses which were sold to other parts of the country, although due to transportation difficulties it was almost impossible to get the rice to good markets. It was the opinion of

American advisers that the rice crop and agricultural production in general ought to be increased. A number of agricultural projects were started, but none of them bore fruit. An irrigation system was developed near the town of Luang Prabang which should have doubled the local rice production as well as increasing that of vegetables during the dry season.

However, once the irrigation system was in use, the technicians discovered that the peasant farmers were not producing a double crop but merely growing the same amount by cultivating half as much land as before. In such a situation it would appear that there was no motivation for economic improvement. A sense of defeatism had developed among the peasantry, as well as among the other classes, in regard to their future and that of their country. Laos had been despoiled by so many outside powers during the past several hundred years that no one, including the peasant, had any faith in its future. If any wealth was accumulated it was put into gold or silver jewelry, which was portable and therefore not subject to the vicissitudes of national fortune. Even the elite of the country followed the same pattern, except that they placed their savings in Swiss or other foreign banks. This pattern of peasants investing in silver and gold and the elite keeping their savings in foreign banks is still widespread in Latin America and Asia. It is an indication of a general lack of confidence in the governments.

Where such a lack of confidence prevails, improvements in the land do not necessarily bring about better conditions for the individual. Where the peasants have had an opportunity to improve themselves economically, and where the government has been relatively stable, as in Thailand, more permanent changes have been brought about. The one sphere of activity in Laos which seemed to be lasting, and where the benefits could not be easily taken away was that of education. In this sphere the peasants were quite willing to cooperate in bringing about improvements. Illiterate fathers had seen enough of the advantages accruing to civil servants and, in general, to those who could read and write to be convinced that their sons should be educated. It was not necessary to sell them the advantages of schooling and they were willing to contribute their own work and materials for the construction of schoolhouses if the state would provide the teachers.

When improvements provide real benefits, villagers are likely to accept them. The profit motive will usually bring about improvements in the growing of cash crops. Where people live primarily by subsistence farming, they often do not have the facilities to grow cash crops profitably. They lack proper transportation facilities or adequate markets, as in Laos or in isolated parts of Africa or Latin America. However, once a region becomes tied to the national or world economy and there are markets to sell the produce, the peasant is likely to accept profitable agricultural changes as rapidly as he learns about them, if he has sufficient land.

A clear-cut illustration of this process comes from the Cayapas River in Ecuador. Here the local Negro population lived in villages on the banks of the river and practiced a subsistence economy based on the growing of corn, manioc, and plantains. In 1948 two fruit companies started a new marketing procedure for bananas, sending regular purchasing boats up the river about twice a week. The farmers had to load their bananas on rafts and canoes and meet the river boats at specified spots, but they were assured a cash market, paying relatively good prices. Bananas began to replace subsistence crops all along the river as far up as the boats could go.[47]

Practical benefit is not only a strong motive in changing agricultural practices but it is also important in other spheres of activity. In nearly every part of the world where a civil service has been developed, people come to value education. They may value it in a narrow sense, simply as a means of obtaining a white-collar job, but this is also true of many Westerners. Most high school and college students in the United States view their diplomas primarily as a stepping-stone to a successful career.

It has already been pointed out that, if a people are convinced that a new kind of medicine or health measure will benefit them, they will accept it. Penicillin is known and used even in remote villages of Latin America and Asia, often injected by people other than doctors. However, the same people may not take to the use of covered toilets because the actual benefit from them is less clear-cut. They know that penicillin brings about remarkable cures, but they find it difficult to comprehend that flies carry diseases transmitted through uncovered human fecal matter.

Thus, in the underdeveloped areas, as in the Western world, obvious, practical benefits are primary in motivating people to accept change. Usually, if innovations are rejected, it is because they were not truly beneficial due to limiting factors in the local culture.

☐   **PRESTIGE MOTIVATION**

Another drive for change is to gain prestige and recognition from one's fellows. In all levels of society there are mechanisms for the individual to obtain the approval of his fellows and very few people attempt to be "islands unto themselves." Most individuals seek approval, which gives them prestige, with the methods their society has defined. In cultures that are technologically simple, such as those of hunting and gathering peoples who do not produce sizable surpluses and a wide variety of goods, men are rewarded for generosity. This is probably the best way the individual can have his self-interest served. Where storage facilities are limited and inadequate, and where little beyond subsistence needs is produced anyway, primitive peoples achieve a form of social insurance by giving to one another in time of need. There are consequently little differences in status in such societies.

Status differences appear as soon as men start producing sizable surpluses and a variety of goods. As these differences emerge, the old pattern of primitive generosity is greatly weakened or lost; in its place, men try to achieve prestige among neighbors. This is not to say that they do not help their neighbors at all, but their prestige status rests more on what they have than what they give to others. Most people attempt to work toward the status position of those above them in the prestige scale. The importance of this fact to development programs is that such people are willing to accept change to achieve better status positions.

A good example of the effect of emulation of others in bettering one's own status position comes from Colombia. In 1952 the Coffee Federation of Colombia provided three million dollars to carry out a hygiene program for coffee growers. It included housing improvements, latrines, a rural water distribution system, and some labor-saving devices for processing coffee. Many of the workers obtained new houses through the fund. The area was surveyed a year later and it was found that the houses near the roads and towns were well maintained. However, within three months, the condition of the houses in remote districts back in the hills was the same as that of the occupants' previous houses. Chickens, dogs, and pigs again had the run of the house; most of the flush toilets were filthy, many of them broken; and crude lean-tos had been attached to the houses to serve as kitchens.[48]

All the farmers were quite willing to receive new houses and facilities; but only those who had houses near roads and towns and were, therefore, in contact with people and conditions of a better class kept them in good condition. This was because their houses could be seen; they served a display function. It is certainly not accidental that when an American has visitors, one of his first acts is to show his guests around his new house. It is his most tangible evidence of prosperity. If no one looked at an American's house, it is doubtful that he would spend so much time and energy in improving it. His motivation is little different from that of the Colombian coffee farmer.

Such Western innovations as refrigerators, radios, and galvanized iron roofing have been accepted widely in the world as status symbols; sometimes they have even been accepted to the detriment of local living conditions. Galvanized iron roofing has been widely adopted in tropical countries although it is often considered far inferior functionally to local materials. In Laos and Thailand, pottery tile used to be the traditional roof covering for Buddhist temples and better houses and wood shingles for the smaller village temples and ordinary houses. When galvanized metal roofing became available, there was widespread use of it on houses, temples, schools, and markets. It was somewhat cheaper to install than tile roofing but, since it lasted a much shorter time, it probably was not cheaper in the long run. In addition, its insulating properties were considerably inferior. When galvanized metal sheets were used in the construction of schools, village people had to build a double roof so as to have a dead air space; otherwise, the rooms were too hot. Tile roofs needed no such extra construction.

The most important factor influencing change through prestige motivation and the emulation of others is *the city*, which serves as a focus of change. In whatever country a change agent is working, the city is extremely important. The outsider will observe that practically all new ideas and devices which enter the country are first funneled through the city. Also, the principal leaders of the country as well as the best educated people of all professions are gathered there. Not much change takes place in the rural areas without having first occurred in the city.

In Greece which, in terms of development, is more advanced than most countries the innovator will work in, city influences move in the following manner. A farmer, who can afford it, sends his son outside the village for advanced education. After graduation the son may become a tax collector, a postal employee, a teacher, or an employee in a bank. He will not return to the village to live, but will visit several times a year, bringing along new ideas and attitudes. His relatives in the village will adopt some new ideas, both out of respect for their urban kinsman and to appear sophisticated. Those who have no city relatives will try to copy those who do. Thus the whole village is affected by city ideas. In one village in Boetia, some of the new ideas adopted in this fashion by the people were city dresses, shoes, toilets and even the practice of going to the hospital when ill.[49]

The level of transportation in a country follows the city in importance as a factor in disseminating new ideas. Changes may enter the city or even be initiated there; but, if the system of transportation is very poor, these ideas cannot get out into the rural areas. For this function, bus systems, railroads, water traffic, and even airplane lines are extremely important. Change will usually be greatest in the urban settlement and radiate in concentric circles into the countryside, becoming weaker the greater the distance. Such change will follow the main transportation routes, the railroad lines, the main highways, or the waterways.

In the last decade, the airplane has been important in bringing new ideas to the back areas, the "boondocks." In Ethiopia, where the roads are poor, the airplane is one of the major factors in the growth of towns and their surrounding areas. Regions around airport towns, many of which were previously almost uninhabited, are now heavily farmed. The river systems of Latin American countries form another such transportation web where the same processes occur. People change their habits through prestige motivation and through emulation of others, and efficient transportation systems allow those in the back areas to communicate with, and to see how those in better circumstances live. The result is that the hinterland peoples' aspirations grow and they become more receptive to change.

The emergence all over the underdeveloped world of *a middle class* is another important factor in change through status seeking. In the United States we have long been familiar with this stratum of society, which includes the majority of our population and is often cited as the economic base and major pacemaker of our country.

Until recent decades there was no such stratum in most areas of the non-Western world. In its place were social systems marked by only two important classes, a small clique of the very rich and a large mass of the very poor. Today, due to the growth of large cities, the development of civil services, and the expansion of mercantile and professional opportunities, an intermediate class has emerged and is increasing both in numbers and in importance. The new middle class consists of urban people, nearly always associated with the new cities. These people have no hereditary status in the old social system, and many of them possess a fairly high level of education, primarily Western oriented. For these reasons, they are often quite amenable to change, hoping through it to improve their individual positions. They unquestionably have more to gain and less to lose through change than any other class, and they are more aware of the kinds of change possible. Moreover, they tend to disseminate ideas throughout society in general more than the groups of any other class.

A good instance of the effect of emulating middle class ideas, even without understanding them, comes from a case study of water-boiling practices in a Peruvian town. A public health nurse worked with 200 families during a two year period on public health problems, trying to persuade them to adopt better health practices. She particularly worked on the problem of trying to get them to boil their drinking water. Of the 200 families, 15 were already boiling their water when she entered the scene. Five of these families boiled their water because they had been influenced by relatives in the city. The women of two other families had worked on a plantation for an upper-class woman where they had acquired the habit and continued it after the period of employment was over. The other eight boiled water because of a local belief that sickly people should not take "cold" foods or drinks, and unboiled water came under this classification. This belief had nothing to do with modern concepts of contamination, since it implied that healthy people could safely drink unboiled water.

The nurse concentrated on another 21 families and in two years convinced 11 more to boil their water. Seven of these 11 families were converted largely because they valued their relationship with the nurse, who was from the middle class of Peruvian society. The other four accepted the new idea after hearing lectures from the public health doctor, also from the middle class, though of a higher rank than the nurse. In none of the conversions did people adopt the new practice primarily because they believed the theory of contamination that the public health people were advancing. In all cases of the water boilers, except perhaps the eight who held the old folk belief that unboiled water is "cold," the individuals who had ac-

cepted the change had been influenced either by city people
or through ideas that had come from the city through the middle class health workers.[50]

Even in India, where the social sciences have been primarily concerned with studies of the traditional castes, the
new class differences also exist. In village India, where the
caste divisions remain strongest, middle class values are nowadays entering the scene and affecting patterns of change. In
a study of a northern Indian village, it was found that the
eight traditional caste groups could be divided into two socioeconomic class groups, lower and middle, the middle class
individuals being those of highest caste. A true upper class
would be found only in towns or cities. These members of the
middle class tended to use scientific medicines considerably
more often than did members of the lower class.

The factors underlying this tendency were threefold: they
were better off economically and could afford the medicines
of Western doctors; they were better educated and consequently more familiar with the newer concepts of disease
control; and they had greater mobility, and could therefore
get to doctors and clinics more easily. The members of this
middle class took trips outside the village more often, at which
times they came into contact with urban-secular values and
practices. Of the sixteen middle class members who had steady
jobs outside the home village, ten were white-collar workers
in the city. In contrast, only two members of the lower class
worked in a city and both had menial jobs.[51] The new ideas
were obviously coming into the village from the city through
people who had middle class ideas and status.

Practical benefits are important motivations for the acceptance of change; but, where such benefits are not immediately
apparent, individuals may change because of a desire for
prestige, in emulation of others with more status than themselves. Cities and transportation systems figure importantly in
such change since new ideas normally come through the cities,
and flow from there down the roads, waterways, and airways
of the nation. In addition the middle class associated with
city life figures importantly in the transmission of change, be-

cause this class is more amenable to change and is instrumental in passing the knowledge on to the lower class.

☐   **EFFECT OF THE YOUNGER GENERATION**

In many underdeveloped countries, the difference of attitude and values between the children and parents is a source of change closely related to that of the middle class. This is also true in developed countries, but less so than in areas which, in a decade or two, are moving from the self-sufficient, traditional society of yesterday into modern nationhood. In these areas, literacy is undoubtedly one of the major factors in creating such a marked difference since, through education, the young are exposed to at least part of the Western body of science and belief.

In the United States the closest parallel of this distinction is that which occurs between immigrants and their children. The immigrants themselves do not, or cannot, always transform themselves into Americans in a lifetime. They cannot eliminate the accents of their native language when they learn English and some cannot even acquire fluent English. Their children, unless in very isolated communities, fully learn not only the new language but also the values and customs of American culture. In the underdeveloped countries, many parents have grown up in an illiterate world which was not much larger than their village areas. Their children have learned something of the new world of nationalism and Western science through the modern educational systems and communications that have at least started to penetrate their societies. They are understandably more receptive to change than the older persons whose habitual cultural patterns are much more deeply rooted.

These differences should be understood in conjunction with the fact that the older generation usually has a greater vested interest in keeping things as they were. A present-day Egyptian village has been described as being basically divided into a younger "revolutionary" faction and a traditional group made up of the older men, the family heads. Until recently the family head had great authority, ultimately based on his ownership of the land and his right to disinherit his sons if they did not obey him. The population has now grown so much that there is not enough land to go around. Therefore, disinheritance has become a weak threat. Another cause of the breakdown of traditional authority has been compulsory education. It has taken the boys from the fields and brought them into contact with many Western ideas; it has also given them a group consciousness. They now challenge the authority of the older men and are willing to champion innovations. Meanwhile, the conservative faction does not easily accept revolutionary proposals and looks back nostalgically at the "good old days."[52]

Motor patterns are particularly hard to change when dealing with older people. In the 1930's, the Mexican government established some trade schools in order to spread the knowledge of labor-saving techniques, including use of the potter's wheel. Some years later it was discovered that in Michoacán villages, where circular motions previously had never been used in the manufacture of pottery, the wheel had not been adopted. The traditional motor patterns of the adult potters had been so deeply ingrained that they either would not take time to or could not master the new technique. In villages where the use of rotary motions was traditional, the wheel was often adopted.[53]

In underdeveloped countries, established cultural habits do not prevent the introduction of mechanical innovations, but ordinarily it is the young who make the jump into the mid-20th century. In practically all countries where automobiles and motorized vehicles have become available, the young men have taken to them with alacrity, becoming not only adept drivers (though possibly incautious by Western standards) but also adequate mechanics. A new motor pattern, such as shifting from right to left-hand drive, is sometimes difficult for Americans or Europeans, since they have normally learned one or the other when they began to drive. The former countries of Indochina inherited from the French the pattern of driving on the right. Thailand, on the other hand, has left-hand traffic, acquired through British influence. Laotian and Thai bus and truck drivers had no trouble at all with this change; they automatically shifted when they crossed the border and accepted this change as an inexplicable but quite manageable difficulty in international relations. Americans from Laos often had near collisions because they could not shake off the habit of driving on the right side when they crossed into Thailand.

Food habits show the same kind of resistance. They are to a large extent arbitrary and defined by culture. Although all members of a culture will resist changes which violate traditional patterns, the young people will be willing to change much more quickly. They will experiment. In India, when tea was introduced in the 19th century, the more conservative elements resisted its use because it was not a traditional drink. A hundred years after its introduction, older people still counseled against excessive use of the beverage, claiming among other things that it caused sterility in males. Nevertheless, tea drinking had become so widespread among the younger people by this time that the counsel of the older people no longer had any effect. The same thing happened concerning milk products in Southeast Asia. Traditionally, the use of animal milk for food was an idea which did not get any further east than India. The people of China did not use milk and the migrants from South China who make up the present day populations of Burma, Thailand, Laos, and Vietnam brought with them a bias against its use. However, in recent years milk and ice cream have been introduced into the cities of Southeast Asia—Hong Kong, Saigon, and Bangkok—and they have become very popular, particularly ice cream. The young flock to ice cream parlors as avidly as do a group of American teen-agers.

In general, changes will be accepted more readily by the young than by the older people. This is true of all cultures, but the phenomenon of the "generation effect" is doubly pronounced in the underdeveloped countries because they are receiving concentrated doses of Westernization and modernization in such a short time. Literacy and education are usually the prime movers in creating this intensified generation effect. Motor habits and food preferences are particaularly relevant to it. The young can and will experiment more easily than the old.

□   **RELIGION AND THE SUPERNATURAL**

As with almost all aspects of culture, religious beliefs can work both for or against change. Innovators often conclude that people of underdeveloped countries are unwilling to change mainly because of the *fatalism* inspired by their religious beliefs. In the simplest terms this means that people believe the events of their lives are preordained and that little can be done to alter them. This is the *karma* of Hinduism and Buddhism, the *kismet* of Islam or "God's will" of Latin America.

There is a great deal concerning human existence that cannot be altered, and if one lacks the scientific explanations and devices available to a Westerner, there is a need to depend on explanations of "fate." Where sudden death is commonplace and the traditional methods of curing are always of doubtful efficacy, an explanation that it was "fate" fills an important gap. In 1953, during discussions with factory workers in India about the size of their family, they often said that they had no need to worry about how many children they had because if God wanted the children to survive, he would provide for them. If it was their fate to live, they would live, if not, they would die. This attitude primarily reflected their inability to be sure a child would live; for so many of them died. Western methods of curing illnesses were neither understood nor sought after; nor were these people in a financial position to go to Western-trained doctors, even had they been convinced of their greater ability to cure. Their economic status gave them little opportunity to obtain more food or clothing for their children. Furthermore, they could not limit the number of births through the various means of family planning that are available to Westerners, because they had no knowledge of them.

"Fate" provided an explanation when they died of sickness or malnutrition.

Fatalism is usually a negative attitude; that is, it more often explains why unpleasant things happened than the reverse. It explains why someone died or why the crop failed, rather than why some person remained healthy or why there was a good crop. It is usually based on realistic facts. A second negative attitude, derived from almost all the great religions, is the emphasis on goals that are other-worldly. An individual gets his reward, not on this earth, but in that afterlife promised by each particular belief.

In this respect Christianity and Judaism are no different from Buddhism or Hinduism or Islam. However, most Christians and Jews work for some worldly goals, and the members of these other religions also do so when they have the same opportunities. Other-worldly goals can be used for explanations, and thus do not necessarily prevent change, if the change is really possible and they truly believe they will benefit by it. In the Egyptian village previously described, which was divided into two factions, the older traditional faction that feared change, because its own position would be weakened thereby, justified its beliefs by the Koran. According to them, God had given to the Prophet Mohammed instructions for the forms of worship and the problems of human survival that were never going to change substantially. The faction of younger men supported Western techniques of social welfare and the new social order in Egypt. Change would benefit them.[54] Fatalism is an attitude to be reckoned with in the underdeveloped countries, but it will probably fade in importance in proportion to the increase in opportunities offered to individuals.

Religion is important to change in two respects. One is that the brotherhoods of monks or priests often have enough power or influence so that projects should be worked out with their cooperation or, at least, without antagonizing them. The instance of the wells in Laotian villages provides a good example of how to work through them. Since there is no consistently cooperating unit in Laotian villages except that of the Buddhist monks, they would have been an excellent group to assume the responsibility of maintaining wells. An example of a failure caused by ignoring the important religious brotherhoods was that of the well project in the Viru Valley of Peru. Here the advice of the Catholic priests was not sought. The local priest had already been critical of modernization because it stressed secular values. When he and the lay religious officials were both ignored during the planning of the well-drilling project, both refused to give it support. It was later suggested that the project might have succeeded if the religious fiesta or the cult of saints had been employed to publicize the well-drilling, and if the site of the well had been blessed by the priest.[55] At the very least, the priest should have been consulted.

The second important aspect of religion relating to innovation is the beliefs themselves. Obviously, one cannot violate the deepest beliefs of the local people and expect their co-operation. Religious beliefs of another culture can set limits to change, but to get a technical innovation accepted, a direct confrontation of religious beliefs is not sensible.

The problem of free-roaming and excessive numbers of cattle often recurs in most village improvement programs in India. Point Four technicians used to concentrate on raising subsidiary crops that the "sacred" cattle wouldn't eat, rather than try to fence them out of fields. In the pilot project at Etawah, the planners wished to upgrade the cattle; but they could not destroy the scrub bulls because killing cattle is opposed to the Hindu religion. However, through patient work with the villagers, the idea of castrating scrub bulls was ultimately accepted. An artificial insemination center for breeding cows was opened because good bulls were not available. This was an even stranger idea to the villagers, but when the resulting calves were seen to be of better quality, many local farmers were encouraged to bring their cows to the center. There were still scrub cattle in the countryside, so the problem was by no means settled, but it was improved.[56] The Hindu belief that cattle are sacred is a very strong one, and anyone who understands Hindu culture realizes that, even if it is eventually bypassed, it cannot be done quickly.

Religious beliefs can often be used in a positive way.

Changes can sometimes be tied in with certain religious practices or justifications for them found in the religious literature and beliefs. In the Etawah project, a village-level worker managed to convince orthodox villagers to try green manuring in their field cultivation by overcoming an initial objection based on religious beliefs. The objection was coming mainly from an orthodox Brahmin who refused to sanction the planting of *san* hemp, the green manure in question, and the plowing of it under as a fertilizer. He objected to such a practice because it was a violent act. The *san* hemp plant was killed and plowed under before it was ripe, in the prime of its life. Moreover, he maintained that Hindu religion taught men not to be greedy, that it was sufficient to fulfill the average needs of the family.

The village worker first argued that even if a plant had a soul, it was immortal and therefore plowing it under would be no sin. He quoted the Bhagavad-Gita extensively, but in this he was no match for the Brahmin. The village worker's arguments failed to convince the Brahmin and his village followers. However, he continued in humility to explain that the farmer's profession was sacred but, in its pursuance, many violent acts had to be committed—that insects and worms were killed in the process of plowing, that green grasses and weeds were rooted out for the benefit of the planted crop, and that the draft animals were forced to work. Yet the farmer did many sacred acts. He fed his family and cattle; supported the temples and priests, teachers, and mendicants; and performed many other acts of hospitality and charity. Without the violent acts necessary to grow his crop he could do none of these good acts. His sins of violence were outweighed by his acts of charity. Moreover, the land was getting poorer each year because of improper manuring. If the green manuring were done, more of the righteous acts would be possible. This argument appealed to the Brahmin and his followers and they finally tried the *san* hemp.[57]

Traditional village life in Greece is permeated by religious acts and beliefs and no important change can take place there easily without the blessing of the Church. UNICEF had a problem in introducing a milk program for Greek children because of religious objections. Milk was forbidden during Lent and the children were required to fast during at least the latter part of that period. However, UNICEF obtained the cooperation of the local bishops on this project, persuading them to drink milk during Lent to show mothers that if it is for a good cause, drinking milk is not a sin.[58]

Religious beliefs constitute both a force for conservatism and a force that can be used as a sanction for change. Fatalism has a religious basis, but it usually reflects the limited possibilities available to the local people. In the doctrines of all world religions there are bases for fatalism, but they are only emphasized where real expectancies are low. Religion can be used positively in two ways: one, in *utilizing the religious brotherhoods and organizations;* and two, in *blending the changes into local religious beliefs.*

☐ **STANDARDS OF PROPRIETY IN BEHAVIOR**

In every culture there are standard patterns of behavior and manners which are considered proper for the individual and which he will be reluctant to violate. If a change is introduced which violates some such standards, it will most likely be resisted. Two aspects of culturally-determined behavior or propriety are particularly resistant to change: personal dignity and modesty. From the Westerner's point of view, a certain change might help the individual a great deal, but if he must act in a way that lowers his esteem in the eyes of his fellows, he is likely to resist the innovation. Adult literacy campaigns have run into considerable difficulties because of this factor. Attending classes is normally considered an activity suitable for children, and adults may object to being seen in this role, even if they wish to know how to read and write.

In the India village development schemes, adult males

who started going to school with a slate and chalk exposed themselves to mild social ridicule. As a consequence, many who registered dropped out. Women with children rarely went, because they thought they were too old to go to school and younger women seldom attended because it was not considered proper for them to be "wandering about."[59] In Ghana, on the other hand, there were plenty of women who took classes, though they rarely took the literacy examinations for certificates. It was believed that they did not show up at the end because they were reluctant to act as equals to men.[60]

Another situation which indicates the problems which can occur when the dignity of the individual is violated has been faced in Indian villages in setting up compost pits. For sanitary reasons such pits were located on the edges of the villages, with the expectation that each family would carry their household wastes and animal manure to them. In the upper castes, there is a fairly strict division of labor between men and women. Carrying manure and household wastes was traditionally a task of women, though they were not expected to be seen carrying it far away from their houses. Consequently, they rarely used the compost pits unless their houses happened to be near them. The women of lower castes were not so bound to their home areas and they did go to the pits. Muslim women, however, who had to obey the rules of female seclusion enjoined by their religious beliefs, were no more free than upper caste Hindus.[61] In this instance, several problems were created because the customary standards of behavior were violated. Men were not supposed to carry manure. Women were, but upper caste Hindu and Muslim women were not supposed to be seen doing this far from their houses. Only the low caste Hindu women could move about freely.

Modesty as well as dignity can create difficulties, and the rules of modesty are often quite different from what a Westerner might consider normal. A consistent problem found in other parts of the world has been the difficulty of getting women to submit to gynecological or other examinations necessary for Western medical practices. The solution usually attempted has been to use women doctors, if and when they are available. Men as well as women can have strong feelings about modesty. Because of a change agent's unwillingness to regard this seriously, his mission failed in Iran. There, men were accustomed to keep the lower part of their body covered even when bathing. They were ashamed to see either themselves or others naked at any time. This was explained to an American sanitary engineer was was installing public shower baths in a local village. The Iranian who explained it told the engineer that the design would not work because the showers were not separated by partitions. The American went ahead anyway, explaining to the Iranian that the local people would have to accept it because there was nothing to be ashamed of, since all men were created alike. But there was no law requiring the villagers to use the bathhouse, and they used it very little, meanwhile joking about the new doctrine of equality.[62]

Until new standards are adopted by the people, their customary standards of behavior and their problems of dignity, pride, and modesty need to be understood. By ignoring them, the innovator will jeopardize his chances of success.

☐ **THE PROBLEM OF COMMUNICATION**

In simplest terms this problem means that a minimum of understanding must pass from the change agent to those receiving the innovation, and vice versa, if success is to be achieved. Usually language barriers create some difficulties. The information passes through an interpreter and, since it is fairly highly specialized, neither the local people nor the interpreter will understand if the innovator is not careful. The interpreter keeps his job on the basis of understanding both languages that are being used. He cannot afford to admit inability to understand either the language or the ideas of the foreign adviser without jeopardizing his position. So his natural tendency is to act as if he understands even when he does not. Secondarily, the specialist is usually a man of high prestige and is assumed to understand far more about his field than the local people, so they may be reluctant to advance any dissenting opinions. The Iranian who voiced his opinion about the public shower baths was probably braver than most local people.

Often vital information concerning the local scene and the particular project does not get to the innovator. A good example of this was the introduction of highly bred pigs and chickens into Laotian villages. The innovator suggested this idea to his local counterpart, who agreed because he believed the American expert understood far more about raising pigs and chickens than he did. However, what the American actually knew was the technique of raising chickens and hogs in a special environment where the animals are given high quality foods and medicines. What he needed to know was the village environment where these animals were going to live. His counterpart might have been able to tell him this, if communication channels had been left open, and if the American had let it be known that he wanted to learn.

Another problem nevertheless remains: the local counterpart also may not be too familiar with situations in the village. Due to the prestige of white-collar work and the gulf that separates villagers from urban residents, officials in underdeveloped countries often do not understand their own rural people too well. In such cases, the change agent will have to get his information through other sources. The point is that communication has to be a two-way process, flowing up to the innovator as well as down to the villager, whether through an intermediary counterpart or without him.

Difficulty in communication is particularly found in health projects partially because of professionalized terminology and procedures and partially because of the high prestige of doctors. This prestige is usually bestowed on the doctor because of his high social position rather than his ability as a curer. In non-Western countries, the patients may not be convinced that the Western-trained doctor is capable of curing all illnesses, or even most of them, but they usually believe him to be an important man. However, if the local people are to be educated in better health practices, they must have confidence, as well as respect, in both the doctor and other medical personnel.

A problem resulting from such a lack of confidence was encountered in a public health center in Santiago, Chile. The center had been set up primarily to spread health education in the community, but it also dispensed curative medicine from clinics staffed by both doctors and nurses. The doctors did little more than their clinic work and the nurses assisted them; but the nurses also bore the main burden of health education, working with the patients at the hospital as well as in their homes. The doctors were concerned with immediate therapy only and had little interest in the patients' reactions. They assumed that the patients would comply with their orders. The patients showed the doctors respect but had little confidence in them. There was little communication between them, so that possibilities for health education were effectively blocked. The nurses were much closer to the patients, acting as their inter-mediaries with the doctors. Consequently, the nurses had gained more confidence from the patients and were in a far better position to provide health education. The director of the center was interested primarily in health education and ultimately took the nurses out of the clinics and had them work full-time on home visiting. The result was a deterioration of clinic practice. The director claimed that it had been counter-balanced by an increase in community health education.[63] The problem was that communication with the doctors was going one way, from top to bottom, but that health education could not take place until it started going the other way also.

It is essential that communication channels remain open. The innovator can properly expect communication to go from himself to the people he wants to help; but he should remem-ber that many of the ideas he presents are difficult to under-stand and accept, and that his own prestige position is high. If he continually communicates, in one direction only, he may be greeted constantly with "ayes"; but noncooperation may actually be growing because the recipients do not know how to reach him with their objections.

☐   **TIMING OF INTRODUCTION**

A well-conceived project can fail simply because the right time was not chosen to initiate it. The change agent should become aware of the daily, seasonal, and periodic work patterns of the people and utilize them in starting and continuing his own projects. Agricultural work periods are particularly critical. A peasant people who are dependent on a staple crop will be unlikely to sacrifice time for something new when their next year's food supply is at stake. The Ghanian village literacy campaign considered this their main problem, primarily because they did not gear their classes to the seasonal necessities. For the 1952 campaign it was reported that the two main occupations in Fantiland (a district in Ghana), cocoa farming and fishing, kept almost all members of these occupations from attending classes between June and December, as well as for a shorter period in the first half of the year. The annual migration which took place for these occupations was considered the largest single adverse factor in the campaign. Similarly, in Trans-Volta, Togoland, after the first two months there was a big drift away from classes by workers on cocoa farms.[64] Such a problem could have been taken care of, at least to a limited degree, by adjusting the teaching periods to seasonal needs.

Good timing can also be used in a positive manner. In a situation where a particular disaster or threat occurs, if the innovators are able to provide a solution, they can gain considerable confidence. Later, this confidence can be built up by taking timely action. It was mentioned that the cattle inoculation program of the Etawah Pilot Project in Northern India got off to a very effective start, because an epidemic of cattle disease was then sweeping the area. At that time, almost 5,000 cattle were inoculated by the village workers and not one died from the epidemic. After this, the number of cattle brought in was greater each year and inoculation was no problem.[65]

Although the innovator cannot count on it, a people who become interested enough in a project may eventually change their seasonal patterns; but they themselves will have to do this. Village projects in Laos were normally considered to be possible only in the dry season. In general, this was so. However, education was so highly valued that when, after nearly two years, the government finally provided the cement and hardware that the villagers had been promised for new schools, they began work on their schools immediately and continued right into the rice-planting season. In many of the villages, when there was a need for the men to be in the fields, the women took over the work of school construction. In this particular instance the drive was so strong that they worked on several buildings nights as well as days.

Timing should always be an integral part of planning. Projects should not be planned for periods when people are occupied in critical work. In addition, an alert change agent will watch for occurrences which will give him opportunities to bring about dramatic improvements.

☐ **CONTINUITY OF PROJECT**

In many parts of the underdeveloped world, administrators and innovators have started projects only to abandon them subsequently. There are even some areas where villagers believe this to be the normal pattern. Such villagers may co-operate as long as the change agents or administrators are around, but will abandon the projects as soon as these advisers leave. Because of this patterned attitude of many villagers, the use of demonstrations and public participation to convince people to accept a new idea was of limited success in northern India. It was not so much that demonstrations or participation were not of value as that there was little continuity connected with them. The villagers had seen agricultural officials give routine demonstrations for the past two decades; although there were considerably more demonstrations during the community development program of the 1950's, the stereotyped attitude toward them remained pretty much the same.

The village developers worked under two handicaps: they

tried to fulfill certain objectives to satisfy their own chiefs, and they tended to work with the important villagers so that the work would progress with less difficulty. Often, they especially tried to finish spectacular projects just before the arrival of important visitors. This may have made the project look good but it was no evidence of any genuine development.

The most important element in change is a change of attitudes in people. New projects can be abandoned as fast as they are developed if the people do not accept them. In this particular instance in northern India the villagers had an established reaction toward development programs. They believed that demonstrations and cooperative work group projects were passing whims of the government which would last for only a few days; therefore, the best thing to do was to go along with them. They also realized that the village developers were government officials who were paid for their work, for which they had to make a showing; so, by obliging them, one could obtain their favor, which might later be of use.[66] However, the soakage pits dug for official visitors would slowly deteriorate after the visit; the compost pits would not be used; and the habits of the people would be little changed.

When a change agent begins a project and then fails to follow it through, not only is his project a failure but he is also building a kind of negative reaction in the people he is trying to influence. When he or his successor returns, he will find an apathy and lack of confidence that will be doubly hard to counteract. No innovator can foresee all the consequences of a projected change, but he can attempt to keep some element of the project going so that it will not become a complete failure. Often over-complicated devices or projects are introduced where maintenance ability is not very high.

The example of the introduction of wells in Laotian villages was one where the maintenance problem was not considered. The technicians simply drilled wells in the villages assigned to them and then departed. The pumps were not so complicated that they could not have been repaired by local people, but none of the local mechanics had been approached and the villagers were given no idea where to obtain help.

They associated the wells with Americans and those villagers that tried to have their wells repaired, came to the local American representative. A small amount of familiarization could have been given to one of the local mechanics and some arrangement could have been made to have a supply of parts available. The local village headman or teacher could have been informed of repair shops where they could go in case of trouble. There were bicycle and motor vehicle repair shops in town where villagers were accustomed to go in case of need; so this would not have been too unusual a step. These particular wells were put in for dramatic effect and in the short run they provided it. Everyone was happy with the water while the pumps worked, but after a year or two, when they were mostly broken and abandoned, they merely served as objects of jokes about the experts. In the long run, it would have been better not to have drilled them.

The only final proof that an innovation has been accepted is when the local people are using it as their own without the advice or prodding of the innovator. One of the most striking examples is that of the Vicos Project in Peru. In 1952, with the support of the Peruvian government, Cornell University took over a *hacienda* in Vicos for research and development. From the beginning, the planners attempted to work on conscious needs of the Indians and to utilize their full participation. This was done in the expectation that the Indians could take over their own local government when the project had run its course. Many achievements were made in technology, economics, nutrition, health, and education. However, the final, most significant development occurred five years later, in 1957, when the adult citizens of Vicos took over control of their new improved community and the Cornell project administrators were able to step out of the picture.[67]

The continuity of a project is necessary both to maintain a positive attitude among the local populace and as the only indication that the innovation has been truly accepted. When the local people no longer need the innovator, he has done his job.

5

THE UNDERDEVELOPED
AREAS

Although the culture of each country in the underdeveloped areas is unique in many respects, there are some characteristics which almost all of them share. This is mainly due
to the fact that they have experienced a common history in
the past 400 years in their relationship to the industrializing
West. Although we know that the nations of Asia, Africa, and
Latin America had their problems and were not utopias before
the appearance of the first Westerners, the problems of today
that make us classify them "underdeveloped" are primarily
a result of the impact of the West. In fact the term "underdeveloped" has relevance only when used in comparison with
"developed," which means the industrial West. It is of no
value to romanticize the past of the underdeveloped areas
before the impact of the West; but it is of value to know that
what took place after 1500 A.D., when the first Westerners
appeared, has shaped their world.

☐   **THE COLONIAL PAST**

The innovations and technical advances that the Westerner
brings have the unfortunate appearance, sometimes at least,
of being self-seeking measures designed for the advantage of
economic exploiters. In the narrowest sense, the innovator is

in the country because of the self-interest of his own country or organization and it is probable that this is generally recognized. However, this form of self-interest requires that he try to improve the conditions in the country where he is working. His success depends to a large extent on the success achieved by that country. In this sense the effort is cooperative, not one way, as has been too often the case in the past.

The particular danger to his program does not arise from the merits or demerits of the techniques being applied, nor from any personal or national dislike toward him or his country. It arises because the weight of the past is against him. The past history of contact between the West and the underdeveloped areas is long and has not always been pleasant. It has given rise to certain important and widespread attitudes which it would be folly to ignore. The innovator must deal with them because they are an inescapable part of the world in which he will work.

Economic development is not something new in the world. The history of contacts between the Western and non-Western countries is strewn with the wreckage of many past attempts to develop these areas. Many of these have been well-intentioned, though in the main, development of the less-favored areas has been undertaken for the clear benefit of the colonizing powers and only secondarily for the benefit of the local people.

The record of colonialism shows a considerable measure of success. Most of the great cities of Asia and Africa were built as trading centers by European powers, and ultimately they became the industrial and administrative centers of their countries. Some, such as the cities of Saigon, Hanoi and New Delhi, remain today as the best designed in Asia. Elaborate transportation systems, such as the railway networks in India and Pakistan, were built by the colonizing powers. Seaports were constructed, industries begun, plantation systems set up, and educational and administrative systems organized in most such countries.

But developments of this kind are inseparable from the story of the discoveries, wars, conquests, seizures, uses and abuses of natural resources and labor, headlong economic booms and busts in raw materials or plantation products, colonization at break-neck speed, and "openings-up" which have filled the period of Western European expansion and which have taken the Westerner to every corner of the earth.

A glance at the history of European colonial expansion over the rest of the world since 1500 gives a vivid picture of the contact between Westerners and non-Westerners. This history reminds us that the inequality between nations which exists today is quite recent and no reflection on the formerly isolated local civilizations that graced Asia, Africa, and the Americas before Columbus. The Spanish conquistadores marveled at the empires of the Aztec in Mexico and the Inca in Peru and compared the cities there very favorably with their own Spanish cities. The products of China and India were in great demand in Europe for their excellence, and this demand was one of the reasons why Europeans strove to exploit these countries.

Even sub-Saharan Africa, which white men once thought dark and savage, now, in the light of modern scholarships, presents a picture of stable and complex native societies. The chaos of the 19th century, before Africa was partitioned by the colonial powers, dates not from time immemorial in a "continent without history." It dates, instead, from the destruction of native kingdoms under the combined onslaught of Arab expansion, European contact, and the slave trade. When one considers Africa's past relationships with the West, one can understand why a country such as the Congo is so turbulent. It has been estimated that, by the end of the 19th century, at least 15 million Congolese had been exported as slaves.

Much of today's poverty and disease around the world is indirectly a product of European expansion. Even the terrible overcrowding of some of the Asiatic, Caribbean, and Middle Eastern countries, which contributes so heavily to today's population problems, is primarily a result of this experience. On the whole, the death rate and birth rate in these countries were stabilized until Europeans brought in relatively simple improvements of epidemic control, transportation, and improved agricultural techniques—thus unintentionally affecting the death rate. As nothing was done about the birth rate, which continued high, these changes by themselves resulted in a rapidly increasing population. Seen properly, all these conditions are part of the complex results of the contacts between Westerners and non-Westerners since 1500.

The common experience of these countries in their contact with the West has been that they have been pushed and enticed, willingly and unwillingly, toward economic and political incorporation with the alien West. Sometimes as colonies, sometimes as free dominions, republics, or unconquered native kingdoms, they have moved toward entry into the community of nations which the Western countries have led. Although the move was not always propelled by overt force, these nations have had little choice.

The pressure to which they have been subjected has brought the destruction of many local values, but it has had its constructive sides as well. The local civilizations outside of Europe before 1500 held much that was very good, but there has been much real progress in the world since then. Transportation provides a vivid example. In areas where 400 years ago people travelled by foot, dugouts, or oxcart, it is now possible to go by train, bus, or airplane. This is a positive kind of improvement which people from these areas recognize as readily as any Westerner.

Whether a people have been independent or colonial in status, whether they maintain still-living ancient civilizations undergoing modernization as in Asia, the Middle East and Africa, or whether they are developing their own amalgams of Western and other traditions as in Latin America, they are alike with regard to pressure from the West. They have been pushed toward conformity to international law, toward production for world markets, toward universal literacy and education, toward control of disease and reduction of mortality, toward nationally-integrated forms of government which, if not always democratic or representational, are based on constitutions and centralized bureaucracies.

Not all this influence has been one-way. The West has received a great deal from the non-Western nations since 1500—

raw materials, valuable minerals, domestic plants, technical ideas, moral and artistic traditions, and people. But the main direction of pressure and power, and the demands for change and conformity, have run the other way. The Asian, African, and Latin American countries have had to accommodate themselves to these pressures, to learn to live with them, and even to resist them when they have become too great. The present-day technical change programs are treading this old path, already marked by the psychological attitudes of a long history of accommodation.

☐   **NATIONALISM**

Every culture tends to be ethnocentric, to regard its own traditions and values as better than those of others. This is as true of the underdeveloped nations as of the developed ones. Beyond holding to this normal ethnocentric viewpoint, however, the people of the developing countries have a strong, emotion-backed drive to achieve a respectable place among nations. It is a place which has been denied them for four hundred years and which, now that independence has been achieved, seems at last possible to win. National aspirations and hopes are universal, but the underdeveloped nations of today are especially intense in their desires to achieve them. However, most of this nationalistic drive resides in the educated class. The majority of these countries are not sufficiently integrated for the populace to share such aspirations. Presumably, nationalistic feelings will spread as literacy increases and communications improve, but in many countries this is not yet the case.

A kind of three-phase cycle has occurred in many such nations. At first the local people resist changes other than material goods and techniques of obvious utility, for they realize that even minor changes may exert strong influences on their culture. Then there is a greater acceptance of the alien ways, particularly by the younger people, because of the realization that these alien ways really do produce superiority, at least in terms of power. The elders and those who try to maintain the old customs are taunted as old-fashioned. There is an urgency to accept the new as rapidly as possible. Then the realization occurs that the local people cannot be full participants in Western culture, largely for economic reasons. Furthermore, the traditional culture reasserts itself.[68]

By this time, the local people have learned enough of the technical superiority of the West to convince them of its advantage, but the non-technical aspects of Western culture may be rejected. There may even be a reassertion of traditional ways in all respects other than the purely technological. In their costumes, language, folklore, artistic styles, sports, and religion, the traditional culture will be emphasized; even an interest in archeology may be fostered as a tie to a glorious past. During the period of colonialism, the reconstruction and maintenance of archeological monuments in India was left almost entirely to interested Englishmen. The famous ruins of Angkor Wat in Cambodia were reconstructed by the French; the Cambodians showed little interest. Now, in India, Egypt, Mexico, Cambodia and Thailand, the local independent governments are greatly interested in the monuments of the past and spend considerable parts of their budgets for the maintenance of such ruins. Cambodia and Thailand have recently ended a long-standing quarrel about the ownership of a ruin which is situated near the border of the two countries. Such ruins are now visible symbols of national greatness; under colonial or dependent status they indicated only more sharply how far their nations had fallen.

Such motivations of nationalism can be understood, but what is less clear is that there is a possible danger to the countries themselves in overstressing their own traditions. Although it is not suggested that the nations of Asia, Africa, and Latin America become "little Americas," there is evidence that some aspects of their cultures, in both the social and religious spheres, will have to change if they are to develop modern industrial economies. Some of the traditions of America and the West European nations were changed in the process of their economic expansion. Similar changed traditions may be a part of the price that must be paid by developing countries, for the achievement of industrial prowess and wealth.

For instance, extended family relationships as a primary method of organizing human relationships are the norm in most non-Western countries, and few of these countries really see themselves accepting the American or European type of family, however much they modernize their codes of law. The individual is controlled in his choice of a mate, his money is absorbed, and the major decisions of life are largely taken within his extended, often joint-property-holding family. It is probably no coincidence that there is a relative lack of initiative and pioneering spirit, and a great amount of nepotism in government and business in such countries. It may be that such a large, joint-property-holding type of kinship unit is contrary to the spirit of saving and investment which has been found so necessary in the West. The individual has no great incentive either to save or invest if he does not derive the benefit, but must share it with many relatives or use it to help support them. Moreover, where such units are dominant, there is a tendency to expend considerable amounts of money for ceremonies and ceremonial giving, as for elaborate weddings and funerals. Such ceremonies cannot be eliminated completely and suddenly because of the risk of deculturizing the population. Nevertheless, to build a situation where capital can be accumulated and investment will be more possible, it may well be necessary to de-emphasize ceremonial expenditures and perhaps even to break up the larger types of family unit.

Even religious beliefs may have to be modified. The puritanical virtues of thrift and hard work may contrast sharply with the traditional generosities of Islam, the other-worldly emphasis of Buddhism, the asceticism of Hinduism, and the fiesta spirit of Latin American Catholicism. It has often been argued that these doctrines are not calculated to produce industrious workers, thrifty capitalists, or daring promoters.[69] To expect the people of the underdeveloped nations voluntarily to abandon their own institutions just to obtain the material improvements of the West is unreasonable, but it is well to recognize that some of these institutions may need to be altered. However, it is more sensible to utilize the drive toward nationalism and national revival than to oppose it bluntly. The fervor of emergent nationalism will seem sometimes shaky, sensitive, and exaggerated. It is nonetheless a potent force that should be considered in all plans for change.

☐ **PLURALITY OF SOCIETY**

National aspirations and hopes are today universal. Remote villagers or awakening tribesmen are now leaving their isolation to establish contacts with the modern world, not simply through direct experience with that world and its people, but through incorporation into a national consciousness as well. National consciousness is abroad in the world today in many different stages of development. In the West that process has for the most part been completed. Most of the countries of Western Europe achieved a unified central national government during the Renaissance and Reformation; the rest, between 1870 and 1918. Their citizens, whatever their local or provincial language and cultural heritage, are today first of all Britons, Frenchmen, or Spaniards in the respective nations.

In the underdeveloped areas, many countries are today in the throes of achieving such national consolidation. Many citizens do not yet know that they are citizens. Many of the societies of the East, for example, are what we call *plural societies;* that is, they contain more than one people, language, religion, or cultural heritage. Sometimes they contain several groups, often extremely different. In a complex country like India there are numerous separate groups. In religion there are Hindus, Muslims, Parsis, Jains, Sikhs, Christians and many different tribal groups. There are over a dozen major languages, each spoken by more than a million people and some by over a hundred million people. There is also a basic and very old cultural difference between the people of the north and those of the south. Finally, the population is subdivided into numbers of caste groups which maintain separate cultural heritages and will not allow intermarriage with other groups.

Even a comparatively small country like Malaya possesses several cultural subgroups—Muslim Malayans; Chinese; Indians, both Hindu and Muslim; and tribal peoples of at least two basic kinds. Such groups may not yet have come to place their common nationality above their particular group allegiance. In India, for example, there have been difficulties ever since its independence in 1947 as to which shall be the national language. This situation is so serious that it has been found expedient to create local official languages as well as the central national language, Hindi.

In some plural societies, where even less national consolidation has been achieved than in India, the different peoples may have no relations other than economic ones. The Burmese, Hindus, Chinese, Karens, and Chins of Burma, lacking common consciousness, make up separate communities of different languages, cultures, and traditions. Remote tribal groups may not only have no desire to become a part of a nation, but also they may not even know there is such a unit. Such people of the hills and of remote areas of secondary importance in agriculture may be quite isolated. Government for them is some kind of outside authority about which they know little and which they want, above all else, to avoid. The shift of their government from colonial to independent status holds very little meaning for them. The remote central authority always exploited them and tried to dominate them; now that their country is independent, the situation is little different than when foreigners were controlling it. Laos is a constitutional monarchy and the king is theoretically the defender of the faith, Buddhism. His symbolic value is far slighter than that of the British queen though, because few people outside of the cities and large towns even know he exists. Certainly the non-Buddhist, tribal peoples know little about him and care less; and in their totality, these people are more numerous than the lowland Buddhist Lao.

The situation is the same in the greater part of Africa which is still partly tribal. The same situation also persisted until recently in the Middle East where separate religious communities have lived under their own laws for centuries, side by side in the same countryside or even in the same towns and cities, though in different quarters. In Latin America the population may be divided between a Spanish-speaking creole or *ladino* cultural majority and several Indian or Negro minority peoples of whom many are still "unhispanicized."

In all these areas the stir of nationalism is now abroad, and the multitude of separate traditions is under attack. In one way or another the emergent, homogenizing nation-states are gathering the diverse people of plural societies into their new, European-derived, integrative, territorial nationalism. The young, the educated, and the internationally oriented seem to be united in the hope of refashioning their world after the national model. Not even the remotest hill tribesmen can any longer escape encroachment on his former free isolation from the centralized, self-conscious government and its enthusiasts.

The new nationalizing central governments, attempting to create unity by binding all the elements of their society together, certainly experience real compulsions. They feel the practical need to utilize the whole of the population of their country toward achieving a position in the world as a strong and wealthy nation. Uncommitted pockets, not integrated into the new whole society, weaken its potential. Then, too, non-assimilated minorities are a constant source of political and military weakness, particularly in the modern context of world power. Agents of political and economic interests from the outside may concentrate their agitation on such unassimilated groups. The central governments use all the customary means of propaganda to reach these groups. They continually try to extend their authority over them, through the appointment of ever more government administrators and the stationing of police and military forces among them—administrative measures today patterned largely on Western institutions.

National school systems are primarily concerned with the dissemination of information about the national goals. Each new nation hopes at least to build a national system of universal education, though few have yet achieved it. Through such schools literacy and the national language can be taught, a means by which the central governments hope to communicate with all groups more easily and by which they hope to better integrate them. By many such nations literacy is viewed as a veritable key to the problem.

In most of these countries, tribal and unassimilated groups are currently being tied to the central government through extensions of the national economy. The remote villages are being tied to the urban seats of central government through new markets, as well as new products, both those manufactured in the cities of the country and those which have been imported from outside. Many such products come to be in great demand. Transportation systems are, of course, vital in such assimilation. New roads, bus lines and railroads make it easier both to get goods to the cities and to travel to and fro. Airplanes also serve this function, and each new country hopes to build a national airways network. Many peoples in Asia, Africa, and Latin America, who have never seen railroads, have become fairly familiar with airplanes. The DC-3 (even if it is privately owned) has become as much a symbol of the central government as the flag or the national anthem. It is no accident that, when governments are overthrown in the underdeveloped countries through revolutionary action, the first thing the new group does is to take control of the airplanes and airports.

□   **THE URBAN ELITE**

The innovater in an underdeveloped country must be ready to cope with another result of the history of the pressures of Westernization. This is the gulf between the educated classes exposed to Western education and the villagers, or other folk, educated in the native traditions. When the colonizing powers took over the countries of Asia, Africa, and Latin America, they created, sometimes deliberately and sometimes accidentally, a group of people that could serve as intermediaries between themselves and the traditional elements of society. At first these people were civil servants employed by the colonizers; but, with the growth of the new cities, expansion of Western-style education, and increasing commercial possibilities, this group of people grew in numbers. The civil servants are still almost all from this class; but nowadays the merchants, politicians, army officers, and even technical specialists are also a part of it.

This is the class of people with whom the change agent will conduct most, or at least a large part, of his dealings; for his own counterpart will be a member. In many parts of the underdeveloped world there is a growing middle class. This class is distinct from the very wealthy, who tended to be the leaders until about ten or twenty years ago. The middle class is still quite small compared to the middle class of the Western nations, but it is growing in influence and numbers. Nowadays it is estimated to constitute from five to fifteen percent of the population in most underdeveloped countries.[70] However, in terms of the whole population of such countries, this middle class can usefully be considered together with the rich as parts of an urban elite contrasted to the traditional rural villagers. The characteristics of this elite set them apart from the villagers, whether they are of the very rich or whether they are middle-income civil servants or merchants.

In the first place, they are urbanized. Almost all live in cities or towns. Their relationship to the rural areas is usually restricted to land ownership. Since there is usually a stigma attached to manual labor, members of this elite rarely do any of the work of cultivation. Those that do own land will have peasant cultivators doing the work, either on a sharecropping basis or as renters.

This elite is comparatively well-educated. Literacy is normal among them and they usually speak the European language of the former colonizers: English in India, Pakistan, Burma, former British Africa, and all the other former British colonies; French in the countries which formerly made up Indo-China and French Africa; Dutch in Indonesia; Spanish and Portuguese in Latin America which has been under intense European influence longer than the other areas. Except for Latin America and parts of Africa the number of people in the total population who speak a European language is small, consisting almost exclusively of city people.

Members of this elite are oriented to a large extent toward the West, because they were educated in a traditional Western fashion and have been under the influence of Western ideas in the cities. They observe many small details of custom learned from the West. Their style of clothing is almost always Western. Men wear shirts and trousers instead of such traditional garments as the dhoti of India, the sarong of Malaya and Southeast Asia and the burnous of North Africa. In all these countries women of the elite class have shown themselves more resistant to change than their men, probably because they have not had as much close contact with Europeans as have the men. Most of them still wear their traditional garments. In the recent post-independence nationalistic fervor, the elite have somewhat reversed this tendency, particularly in the new African nations and a few of the Asian ones. That is, they (usually the politicians) deliberately wear the traditional garments to assert the individuality of their culture.

Elite food habits and patterns of consumption reflect Western influence. They may still maintain their traditional dietary habits at home, but they are also familiar with and use some Western foods and drinks. This is partially an economic factor, but it is partly due to the fact that they are the ones of their country who have learned Western practices. It was mentioned earlier that a considerable amount of milk is now consumed in the cities of Southeast Asia, an area where traditionally people drank no milk at all, and an area where the rural peasants never before milked their cows or buffaloes. The pattern of alcoholic consumption has also changed. Village people all over the world make and drink some kind of alcoholic beverage such as palm or maguey wine, rice or millet beer, local rum, or rice whisky. The city elite now tend to consume standard beers and whiskies made in their countries from European formulas, or imported beverages if they can afford them. Scotch whisky and French brandy are now preferred drinks among the elite in many parts of the underdeveloped world.

Another significant element of the difference between the urban elite and the rural peasant is that it crosscuts cultural divisions based on ethnic differences. For instance, the urban members of various religious groups in a country like India—Hindus, Muslims, Parsis, Sikhs, and Christians—will have a considerable number of cultural habits in common which will place them together in contrast to the rural people of the same religious groups. Hindu, Muslim or Sikh civil servants in a city like New Delhi may well have as much in common with one another as they have with villagers of their own religion.

Although the elite class is a minority group in the total population, from this class are drawn the political, military, and commercial leadership of each country. They are the planners and organizers and the contact men with the West. However, one of the important problems of the developing countries is that, compared to the West, the numbers of adequately trained leaders are pitifully small. This is because independence has come on most of these nations suddenly and, under colonial rule, the present elite had little opportunity to do more than subordinate jobs. A second major problem is that the elite have little contact with and often do not very well understand the rural peasant. This situation is also a carry-over from the colonial days, although it seems to be changing somewhat. This is because the leaders of the newly independent countries realize that the peasant will have to be fully incorporated into the national life, if their nations are to succeed.

☐ **THE RURAL PEASANT**

If a country has 50 percent or more of its working males engaged in farming and related pursuits, it is considered to have an economy based on agriculture. Such agriculture has been termed *archaic* to differentiate it from the mechanized form found in countries that also have a considerable industrial output. About three-fourths of the world's peoples, almost all of them in the tropical or subtropical zones, still have an economy based on this archaic form of agriculture. In the countries where these peoples live, only about ten percent of the population is in cities, just the reverse of the situation in the United States, which has only about ten percent in farming.[71]

The peasant village of today is a type of social unit that has existed since the rise of the first cities, over five thousand years ago. It is not the same thing as an independent tribe, such as those of most North American Indian groups previous to their dissolution and incorporation into Anglo-American national life. Historically it has been the agricultural producer on which the wealth and power of the central cities was built.

Although possessing some degree of self-sufficiency, considerably greater than that of the farmer in an industrial society, the peasant village has been dependent on the city for specialized goods. The city was and is the focus of trade, commerce, and manufacture; what the peasant needed that he could not make himself he obtained from the city or its agents. There was a two-way relationship: the village depended on the city for specialized goods and the city depended on the village for its agricultural production. The peasant developed an ambivalent attitude toward the city. He wanted many of the good things that could be had only through city contacts, the manufactured things that money could buy; at the same time he tried to avoid the exploitative tentacles of the city, the tax collector, the money-lender, and the corrupt official who preyed on him whenever he had the chance.

In contrast to the urban elite, the rural peasant is oriented toward traditional values and customs. Because the average villager is illiterate and his level of education quite low, he knows comparatively little of Western ways. He cannot even take advantage of most of the new devices he learns about, because his economic circumstances are so poor. The average villager speaks only his own language, follows traditional dietary patterns, and has his own medical practices and practitioners. His knowledge of the world is usually confined to the immediate region around his village. Such ideas as he may have concerning the new nationalism have come to him through communication channels controlled by the elite.

Even with the best of intentions, the elite have difficulty in establishing good contacts with the villagers because the gulf between the two groups is so wide. The speeches given by village development officers in northern India were rarely accepted at face value. The peasants would promise to support an officer at the time of his speech, but after he left they would analyze and dissect what he had said from all points of view, particularly in terms of his supposed hidden motives. Then the peasants would react more on a basis of their personal relationship to the individual than on the merits of his program. The language, symbols, and appeal of speeches formulated by the elite often had little meaning to the villagers.[72]

The technology of the peasant is primitive and he is usually a non-productive farmer. If the agricultural year has been good, he produces enough to get by on and some little surplus which he can sell to the town market to buy the few special goods that are not available in the village: a bicycle, a galvanized bucket, some factory-made cloth, some religious objects. If the year is bad, he may have no surplus and even lack the necessary food to last the year. Then his only recourse is to go to the moneylender. Even peasants who are relatively well-off use their extra wealth in a nonproductive, traditional manner. They hoard it, usually in the form of gold or silver jewelry or vessels used in religious worship. They are either unaware of banks, or do not trust them because they are institutions controlled by the city man.

The social group the peasant depends on above all others is that of his family and kin. He is tied to this group economically, socially, and ritually; and it constitutes his insurance company. When people in such kin-based societies do travel, it is characteristic of them to stay only in the houses of kinsmen. In India, the hotel is a Western innovation and is used primarily by Westerners and the Indian elite. Most Indians who patronize hotels in India can speak English. In its common usage, the word "hotel" in Hindi means a restaurant rather than a place where one can find lodging. The Indians learned of hotels from the British but having no need for such an institution in its primary sense (a place to sleep) they adopted its secondary meaning (a place to eat).

When he cannot depend on kinsmen in his relationships, the peasant tends to depend on people he knows well in a personal way or on the basis of face-to-face contact. He does not understand impersonal relationships and he initially distrusts the stranger. This is another result of the peasant's long history of exploitation by people who almost always came from the outside, as often as not from the city. However, even within the village, there is often much distrust and struggle between factions. The main explanation advanced for noncooperation between peasants is that the "economic pie" is too small to be divided; consequently one man's gain is another man's loss. Resources, particularly land, are limited and the techniques for production are simple; production is constant but just barely adequate. Therefore, the peasant regards another man's success as made at his expense.[73] This is the prevalent situation in areas where the population is high and land scarce. In areas where land is not so scarce—most of Southeast Asia, Negro Africa, and the less densely settled parts of Latin America— competition is not as fierce.

The rural peasant tends to be oriented toward his traditional religion far more than the urban elite. Secularization has developed along with Westernization and is largely confined to the cities. The rural peasant supports his mosque, Buddhist or Hindu temple, or church (where there have been considerable conversions to Christianity) as a vital part of his life. He also supports a large body of folk beliefs which are not necessarily part of the orthodox tenets of his religion—beliefs in spirit possession, nature spirits, disease caused by malevolent spirits, and so on. He has not been exposed to enough outside ideas to seriously question many of these beliefs. Experimentation with new ideas is still largely a city phenomenon; many more new ideas take root in the cities than in the peasant community.

☐   ## THE ECONOMY

Most of the nations toward which assistance is directed are underdeveloped in two principal ways—in the inefficiency of their agricultural practices and in their lack of industry. Primarily, there is a need and desire in all such countries to increase the insufficient productivity of their village farmers.

Secondarily, these nations lack sufficient industry for their needs in terms of 20th-century expectations. In some nations that have very recently obtained their independence, industry is practically non-existent.

For instance, in 1961, the only establishments in Laos that could be called factories were a cigarette packaging plant and a soft-drink bottling plant. Practically all these nations aspire to industrialization; but the difficulties are many. Among the major drawbacks are the dearth of working capital and the dearth of incentive, either for the inhabitants or for outsiders, to make local investments. In any case, industrialization alone will not solve the problem of greater food production, a lesson sadly learned in recent years by a number of countries, notably India, China and even Russia. Today the largest countries push a two-pronged effort of development, directed toward improved agricultural production and increased industrialization.

One particular problem that continues to plague non-Western lands is the continuing coexistence of the old and new economies. The old economies may continue to exist, much changed by Western contact, but still operating fairly independently alongside the economic institutions of the new world market. Although the peasant village, by definition, was never entirely self-sufficient, even before the period of Western expansion, it was nearly so; and its economic ties were mainly limited to the cities of the nation of which it was a part. As a relatively self-sufficient, kinship-based, traditional society, such villages differed considerably from the type of rural community with which Westerners are familiar. Even today, the old type of economy may still rule a good part of the lives of people upcountry, in the "boondocks." At the same time, the educated class and the planning officials may be completely absorbed in developing new national industries, international trade, and the new kinds of skilled and unskilled manpower needed for industrial cities.

For instance, the native Indian village communities in Mexico have persisted beside the spreading plantations under foreign and absentee ownership. When rubber cultivation was introduced to Indonesian and Malayan village farmers, they were able to keep pace with the production of the great Dutch and English rubber plantations until Japanese conquests cut off the world rubber market in World War II. Similarly, in the world markets for chocolate and soap, the cocoa and palm oil farmers of West African forest villages are themselves the proprietors who contract directly with large industrial concerns such as Lever Brothers.

In nearly all the underdeveloped areas, there are economies based on subsistence or petty surplus crops intertwined with economies based on standard cash crops produced for national and international markets. Tribal, village, kinship, or religious groupings—not economic interests, or administrative and political divisions—are still, for many people in such areas, the real lines of their affiliations, loyalties, interests, and influence. However, the incorporation of their nations into the modern world has given rise to organs of central government and has caused networks of economic influence to be developed by plantation owners and landlords. It has created credit-granting merchants and moneylenders, agents of foreign mines and mills, and shipping centers. From the national capitals and trading centers, the economic interests of the educated elite now finger out into the villages.

Nonetheless, the forms of government, business, and the professions that Westerners easily recognize are new to villagers; they are novel, alien or urban influences. In Southeast Asia and Africa, for example, the first local representatives of a monetary economy are usually shopkeepers and traders. They are often Chinese, East Indian, or Syrian immigrants serving the native populations of the plural societies that are now typical in these areas. The educated officials, merchants, plantation or mine operators, and the trained professionals practicing the recognized Western-type professions, may be either native or foreign-born—sometimes of the local race, religion, and culture and sometimes not. It does not make much difference; these men of the new occupations are the intrusive agents of a world economy and world civilization pushing their way into the old cultures or the surviving village economies.

There was undoubtedly much that was good in peasant

village life before the impact of the Western-derived institutions and the international economy, but the situation should be assessed realistically. The surviving subsistence economies, tribal and village ties, and ethnic and religious groupings have deep roots and command strong allegiance; but the old way of life of which they were a part is disappearing. Neither we nor they can turn back the clock. The elite will be satisfied with nothing less than a standard of wealth and economic conditions approaching that achieved in the West. Today, even the villagers have had enough contact with outsiders so that they, too, want the advantages which the world economy can bring them, even when they smart under its disadvantages.

☐ **RISING EXPECTATIONS**

There is every evidence that men in all stages of culture and history have been interested in acquiring whatever would benefit them in a practical way, but the desire for such improvements was probably never at such a pitch, on such a worldwide scale, as it is today. Satisfaction with the old way of life, at least as measured by material goods and wealth, is rarely found in the modern world. This statement may seem to belie the fact that people often do not accept improvements brought to them from the outside, even though the innovator is convinced that such changes would be of direct benefit to the people. In most cases when the local people reject an innovation it is not because they do not wish to better themselves.

In Laos when the local people were reluctant to grow surplus rice or vegetables for public sale, many change agents assumed this to be due to a Buddhist complacency with the prevailing conditions of life. The same explanation was often advanced when the Cambodians failed to respond to new ideas. It is true that there was no immediate need for change in either country, since both were underpopulated and people did not have to compete for land, since it was not in short supply as in the densely populated countries such as India or Pakistan.

There were many other powerful deterrents against change

in Laos. To begin with, markets and transportation were poor. Then, the seemingly endless state of political instability made the future unpredictable; in particular, no one could count on keeping land long enough to derive full benefit from efforts to improve it. The Lao would not invest in their own territory for the same reason that a foreign investor will not invest funds in an industrial or agricultural project in a country marked by political unrest. The difference is that the foreign investor can keep out of such a country completely, while the peasant must stay and exert himself at least sufficiently to provide for his family's necessities.

In the two hundred years before the French came to Laos, it had been the scene of one military raid after another. Several invading armies razed whole cities and carried off much of the population. During the several decades of the French occupation, a greater rule of peace was established than the Lao had seen for a long time. Under the new peace, hopes began to rise to a certain extent and new agricultural projects were undertaken. In South Laos, the French built a new 50 kilometer road, traversing a rich plateau. In this area the French introduced new crops and agricultural methods; and the Vietnamese, Lao, and tribal Kha farmers soon followed suit. Coffee, pineapple, corn and temperate-zone vegetables could be grown as cash crops. There was a fairly good road for marketing and the soil was rich.

The French colonial period ended just when the agricultural economy had started to boom. Once again there was political chaos, as bad if not worse than the previous chaos. Not only did transportation suffer, but also markets were affected. It even became unsafe to be in the fields, for fear of being captured by guerillas or units of the royal Laotian army. One after another the newly developed farms were abandoned, reverting to the bamboo forests from which they had been cleared. The Lao were caught up in the wave of rising expectations that has swept most of the world's people, but to meet these expectations through increased agricultural production had become impossible. The Lao wanted bicycles, radios, good imported cloth, sewing machines, and all the other new devices about which they had learned in recent decades; but there was just no practical way for ordinary villagers to obtain them.

One of the most dramatic examples of the growth of such new desires has been documented in the South Pacific, on the island of Manus. In 1928 anthropologist Margaret Mead made a study there of a tribal people who were living in houses built on piles in the sea, and wore little clothing except loin cloths. They settled their disputes by magic curses, and their religion rested on a type of ancestor worship that required them to store the skulls of ancestors in their houses. The Manus had no remembered history, and no knowledge of geography beyond the narrow confines of their island archipelago. They lacked a writing system and their knowledge of political arrangements was only elaborate enough to unite two or three hundred people.[74]

When their new desires took shape, the Manus were already learning of the outside world through missionaries and through plantation owners for whom some of the men worked. However, their first large-scale and intensive contact with the Western world occurred when a large occupation of American military forces established themselves in their region. It was then that they first saw the elaborate equipment of the West. The Americans knocked down hills, blasted channels, smoothed out airstrips, and tore up miles of brush. The Manus experienced a new kind of social relationship. They found themselves treated in a new democratic way which they had never before experienced. Instead of being treated as "boys," as had been the case on the plantations, they were treated as "good Joes."[75]

When the Americans left, the Manus were a changed people. They had experienced such a growth of needs that they decided to remodel their culture. By 1953, when Dr. Mead returned, they had moved their village to the mainland and were attempting to landscape it. (They even gave up pigs because they littered the village too much.) They were now committed to Western concepts of law and police force, they were caring for the old and sick and educating their children. The Manus even discarded the cult of ancestor worship and replaced it with their own version of Christianity.[76] The skulls of their ancestors had been tossed into the sea.

This case has special interest because of the unusual rapidity of the Manus' growth of expectations and their efforts to meet them. Most non-Western people cannot be expected to go so far so rapidly, particularly if they are a segment of an important national culture. In such countries there will be more of a tendency to retain some traditions of the past, certainly religious beliefs. It would be most unlikely for Muslims, Hindus, and Buddhists to give up their traditional beliefs just for the sake of material goods or material well-being, but they will exert themselves as much as possible in other ways to obtain these benefits.

The growth of expectations is intimately connected with communications. If the Manus islanders had never seen the American soldiers it is unlikely that they would have moved so fast. In most cases, such rapid growth of needs will be found in the cities, principally because city people are the first to learn of innovations and can more readily acquire them. People who live in remote areas will be influenced largely by observing the mode of living of urban or urban-oriented individuals. In one community studied in Sonora, Mexico, the people of the wealthiest class in the towns built the best houses and procured the best house furnishings, including air conditioners. A second class of less wealthy people imitated the wealthiest ones, though on a more modest scale. Still a third class, the laborers, were unable to buy most of the objects they saw among the classes above them. Even in small towns, there was an effort to obtain modern conveniences, for they had become powerful new symbols of status. Refrigerators and stoves were purchased even when the houses had dirt floors, which meant that a section of them, just large enough to hold the appliances, had to be cemented.[77]

In this Mexican community, the country people did not change as much as the others. This was not only because they were economically unable to do so, but also because they heard less concerning the latest conveniences available. Another contributing factor was that they felt somewhat inferior, because a large percentage of the country people were of Indian ancestry and lacked the self-confidence of the non-Indian Mexicans. Even so, only the lowest group of Indians would still strive for status in the traditional manner, by taking part in Indian ceremonials and emphasizing their "Indian-ness." Those who had sufficient land of their own attempted to emulate the better-off townsmen by acquiring good houses, radios, sewing machines, sets of living room furniture, gas stoves, and trucks.[78]

☐   **POPULATION PRESSURES**

The expansion and influence of the West have indirectly caused population problems in the underdeveloped countries. The death rate in such areas has been affected through simple technological innovations which have reduced the likelihood of famine and disease. Such innovations include improved methods of transportation and food production and basic public health measures such as insecticide spraying and improving the water supply. In some countries, regular health and medical facilities have been established, where people can get relatively inexpensive treatment. As a result of all these innovations, the death rate has continued to drop, while the birth rate has remained high. Previously in such areas, the high birth rate barely kept pace with the high infant mortality which, combined with the ravages of death, disease, famine, and war, served to balance the numbers of people. A large number of children was necessary just to keep the population from decreasing, and large families were rewarded by society.

For instance, in India, married women had very little status and respect until they had produced a child, and early marriage was customary because it increased the probability of large families. Furthermore, ritualistic beliefs required a man to have children not only to conduct his death rites and perform posthumous ceremonies for him, but also because the continued maintenance of the family land required sons to assume responsibility for and to inherit it. This situation worked out satisfactorily as long as the birth and death rates were fairly well balanced. However, each new technical advance meant that more and more infants survived. Meanwhile the birth rate remained the same, so that population figures went up and up.

An ever-increasing population is one of the general problems of the underdeveloped areas. The countries of Western Europe are densely populated; some, such as Holland, Belgium, and England, are much more densely populated than most nations of Asia and Africa. However, these Western countries are industrialized and wealthy by world standards. It is in non-Western nations, where the smallest present utilization of resources and least per capita wealth are found, that population pressures have become critical. It is one of the consequences of incorporating organized commerce, public health and disease control into the world at large.

In the past there seem to have been "cycles of population growth" based on technological innovations. When technological change takes place, there is a sharp upswing in the rate of population growth followed by a leveling off to a more stable, slower rate of increase or a virtual balance of birth and death rates. The populations of England, Germany and the United States went through such a cycle during their agricultural and industrial revolutions. With the increased food and materials made available by these revolutions, the populations rose rapidly, the birth rate remaining high at the same time that the death rate came down. However, at the end of the cycle the birth rate also came down, as large families went out of fashion.

The demographers predict such a cycle for the underdeveloped countries of the world. They can place a country in the proper phase of its cycle and predict the next phase it can be expected to pass through. For example, both giant India and little Puerto Rico are far along in the stage of population explosion. Mexico and Samoa are in their early stages with the greatest burst yet to come. The population rate in Japan is still rising, but with the acceleration of industrialization and Westernization, its rate of increase is already slacking off. It is significant that Japan is the one nation of Asia that is not in the underdeveloped class.

A growing population can mean greater opportunities but it can also mean more problems. We are not concerned here to take part in the great debate about solutions or to succumb to the wilder fears about "overpopulation," but rather to point out the problems. Growing numbers of people mean more crowded villages. This means that more and more flocks and herds must run on the pastures, and that more and more intensive cultivation must be practiced on the already tired, eroded soil. Cultivable land becomes scarcer as it is subdivided among the heirs in each generation.

A particular problem for the innovator arises from the fact that people with little land but many mouths to feed cannot afford to take chances, to experiment with a new crop or new technique. One crop failure can result in famine. This means that more and more children have to leave rural areas to look for jobs in crowded cities where there are not sufficient jobs for those already there. It means that production for a market forces subsistence food production to give way to cash crops. This in turn means more and more dependence on money and imported, store-bought foods for people who until yesterday often knew only local foods and local self-reliance, and who knew nothing of credit or debt or the vitamin deficiencies of long-stored foods. It means increased poverty at a time when these nations need a surplus for capital investment.

Another result of population pressures is more and more building, expanding, and filling up. People who were once strung out along the rivers and spread across the plains or bush will be huddled into shacks and compounds that spring up along new railroads and near the great new mines, or beside the loading platforms of the great plantations. The commons and protective sanitary open spaces around the villages will be eliminated. The West had its day of slum-building and is still fighting its way out. The underdeveloped areas are just entering their periods of great expansion when such conditions occur.

It is to be hoped that these developing countries can profit by the experiences of the West so that they can avoid the ugly features that marred the urbanization and industrialization of the West. It is hopeful to note that the nations of the non-Western world with the densest populations recognize their problems. Japan, India, Pakistan, Puerto Rico, Egypt—all nations of dense populations—have set up government bureaus and administrative machinery to cope with the problem of family planning, primarily to limit the number of births per family.

6

AMERICAN
CULTURAL VALUES

☐   **MISINTERPRETATION**

In order to incorporate techniques from one culture into another one it is very important to understand the role and background of the innovator concerned. In this manual, several of the cases indicate that an innovator's failure was due to a misinterpretation of the motives and needs of the recipients. Such misinterpretations may rest on the innovator's failure to learn enough about the receiving culture; but they may also rest on false presuppositions, derived from assuming that conditions taken for granted at home also exist in the foreign situation.

It is true that men of all cultures, developed or underdeveloped, have much in common in the solution of their problems. A peasant farmer in India and a Texas corn farmer are both pragmatic and must be shown that an improvement is genuine before they will accept it; and a Laotian farmer tries to get help from the supernatural in producing unpredictable rain just as Americans turn to prayer in an unpredictable situation, such as the disappearance of an astronaut while re-entering the earth's atmosphere. Nevertheless, it still does not follow that all the basic assumptions of people with different cultures are the same. Although we may say that men everywhere are basically alike, the unlikenesses are still significant enough to block communication and thus impede change. If the innovator expects the people of the recipient culture to have precisely the same motivations as he or his countrymen, or to make the same distinctions of behavior, thought, and value, he is seriously risking failure of his plans.

The worst part of such a misapprehension of cultural realities is that it is unintentional. The individual does what is "natural" or what makes "common sense." He may not realize that his "natural" tendencies to action and decision are inevitably limited by his own cultural experience and by unconscious assumptions, based on the way of life of his own people. To examine the cultural premises of one's own actions and thought is a difficult process. In one's own culture it may never be necessary and most people probably think more freely and act better without ever doing it. However, in dealing with people of another culture, it is a necessity of the first importance.

In many of the cases in the previous chapters failures resulted from false presuppositions. Hybrid corn grown by Spanish-American farmers in Arizona was superior in terms of the Anglo-American economy. The innovator assumed that the value of corn was the same for Spanish-Americans as for Anglo-Americans, a false supposition. They valued it more in terms of taste and texture as human food rather than as animal feed. The United States administrators of the Pacific island of Palau assumed that if individuals participated in an American system of voting and electing public officials, democracy would thereby be absorbed into the culture. However, the Pacific islanders defined leadership quite differently than did Americans, and they had an imperfect understanding of the meaning of democratic elections.

In both of these cases the situation was not due to stupidity, but rather to the cultural blindness of the planners who were not aware that they needed information both about themselves and the people they wanted to help. Reliance was mistakenly placed upon "natural" and "common sense" assumptions relevant to the American scene, but inadequate in contacts with people of another culture.

Culture and professional specialization create unconscious blinders for all of mankind. Americans are prone to distortions arising from American attitudes; specialists are prone to be inattentive to whatever their expert training has led them to define as irrelevant. Experts are usually single-minded and specialized. When Americans deal with problems set against the known background of their own culture, specialization has resulted in great strength; but it has been gained only by training individuals to concentrate narrowly. However, in dealing with the problems of another culture, the conditions no longer arise from a familiar background and cannot be taken for granted. People no longer act "naturally."

The American specialist should be given some opportunity of knowing himself as a product of American and Western culture. He should be required to have some understanding not only of the behavior and values of the recipient peoples of foreign cultures, but also of his own assumptions and values. He needs to become aware of unconscious presuppositions from his own culture that tend to influence his decisions and actions in introducing new ideas. He should discover what his probable reactions will be to the difficulties he may encounter among the people with whom he will be working. In short, he needs to know how being an American may help or hinder him in his mission.

The social and psychological sciences, including cultural anthropology, can contribute to the knowledge required. They give a fairly adequate portrait of "the American character," as exemplified by most Americans.

The United States, like any other country, has a national culture. All people born and raised in this country have been strongly conditioned by it. This does not mean that they will all be alike, or that if some act differently from others they are more or less American than the others. It does mean, however, that among Americans of all regions, national origins, races, classes, and both sexes, there are some points of likeness in acting and thinking that turn up more frequently than among groups of people in other countries. The following characteristics will be drawn primarily from classes of the middle levels of income and status. It is from this sector of the population that most change agents are drawn.

The characteristics of American character have been traced to many sources. The values derived from life on the frontier, the great open spaces, the virgin wealth and the seemingly limitless resources of a new world appear to have affected our ideas of freedom. Individualism has been fostered by the inventive spirit and technical advances of the country, the successful expansion of capitalism, and as a result of the huge, free mass market. Much of our religious and ethical tradition seems to have been derived from Calvinist (Puritan) origin. We inherited Anglo-Saxon civil rights, rule of law, and representative institutions; the ideas of egalitarian democracy and a secular spirit sprang from the French and American Revolutions. The melting pot, the staggering trans-Atlantic migration of Europeans for over three centuries, has affected our national character. All these, and many other historical circumstances, have gone into the making of the modern American character.

It will be useful to describe some of the most important features of American culture, as one of the "developed" countries, in order to make clear the contrast with most of the "underdeveloped" countries which have been described previously. We make the contrast not to exalt our own conditions or belittle those that prevail elsewhere but to show why American assumptions differ from those of many other peoples. The contrast is based on facts. The conditions we picture hold good not only for the United States but also, to a large degree, for other developed countries—most of Western Europe, New Zealand, Canada, Australia, and some of the countries of South America. Many of these countries have had an historical or economic development similar to that of the United States; although none show the particularly American combination of cultural features.

☐   **AMERICAN CULTURE**

The culture and people of the United States, then, have some special characteristics. Compared with other countries, the number of people is considerable, though they are spread rather thinly over a huge area of many diverse natural environments, most of which are rich, temperate, and still not intensively exploited. Americans command an exceedingly rich technology and a wealth in manufactured goods that is now the greatest in the world. The consumption rate of these goods is also high.

Although the country has a strong agrarian tradition in which farming was a family specialty, and though farming still produces an extraordinary yield of foodstuffs and fibers, the nation has become urbanized and dominated by its cities. The farming population consists of less than ten per cent of the total and agriculture has become so mechanized it can now be considered as merely another form of industry. Daily living for the majority is characteristically urban, regulated by the clock and the calendar, rather than by the seasons or an agricultural cycle. People live on money rather than on subsistence goods or property. They are mainly employees living on salaries paid by large and complex impersonal institutions. Money is the common denominator of exchange, even property usually having a value only in terms of its monetary worth.

Because of the high standard of living and the high level of technology in the country, people have long lives. Their birth rate is also low, but their death rate is one of the lowest in the world; and this keeps the population from expanding as rapidly as in some of the underdeveloped countries.

Americans are a comparatively new group of people with a short history. Their origins are among the most diverse of the entire world, with a continuing variability of racial and ethnic stocks and a profusion of minority groups.

Americans exhibit wide ranges of wealth, property, education, manners, and tastes. Despite these diversities of origin, tradition, and economic level, there is a surprising conformity and almost continent-wide uniformity of language, diet, hygiene, dress, basic skills, land use, community settlement, recreational activities, use of mass communications, and innumerable other activities. The people share a rather small range of standard moral, political, economic, and social attitudes, being divided in opinion chiefly by their denominational, occupational and ethnic (race and national origin) interests. There are some regional variations, though these do not amount to a plurality of social views in the same sense as in some of the underdeveloped countries. There is a high degree of mobility, both geographically and occupationally.

There are status differences in America, based mainly on occupation, education and financial worth. Although in theory all persons have equal opportunities, there are certain limitations, particularly those based on racial or ethnic grounds, beyond which it is difficult for some individuals to go. Although a Negro may be appointed as a member of the Cabinet, it is improbable that one could become President and it is difficult for one to be elected to either house of Congress. Despite these limitations, most people change jobs, move from one city or region to another, or move up or down in status level with great frequency. They do not seem to mind being uprooted, a process so painful in other countries.

Husband, wife, and children constitute the basic American kinship unit, the nuclear family. There are high marriage rates, the couples setting up their own small households. Unlike many people in the underdeveloped areas, Americans have comparatively few children and rarely spend their lives as part of larger households. Family relationships are fluid and not particularly stable. Nowadays divorce is common and family custom usually requires old people and unmarried adults to live apart from their kin. In place of strong kinship ties, people tend to rely on an enormous number of voluntary associations of common interest, which they join—parent-teachers associations, women's clubs, social fraternities, church clubs, recreational teams, and many others.

The general level of education is high; literacy is high but by no means universal. From the age of six to sixteen the child is in an academic institution, learning the goals of good health, good character, and good citizenship. He is also taught to be competitive and adaptive to changing environments. He learns basic standard skills (driving cars, basic mechanics, reading,

writing, arithmetic, typing, the liberal arts) rather than hereditary specializations. Specialization comes later in professional
training.

The moral tone of the country is heavily Calvinist Protestant, but there are many other sects of Christianity. The religious beliefs are concerned almost as much with general
morality as with man's search for the afterlife. Family relations,
sexual customs, man's relationship to other men, and civic responsibility are all concerns of religion. A puritanic morality
has become generalized and secular, part of the culture rather
than the code of any single religious sect. No religious group
is supported by the state. Formal religion is compartmentalized
as are many other aspects of American life. A high percentage
of the Protestants who form the bulk of America's population
attend church sporadically and infrequently; and religious
ideas seldom are mixed with secular ones. The church serves a
strong social function, being the center of many clubs and
groups. Religion is not a particularly unifying institution in
American life. The spirit of the country is increasingly secular
and rationalistic. It is not antireligious or even anticlerical, as
is so often the case elsewhere; it is rather a spirit of religious
indifference. The majority of individuals simply do not concern
themselves with religion in the conduct of most matters.

The implication of this thumbnail sketch of American culture should now be clear. Neither the American complex of
cultural conditions nor most of its important particulars can
be relied upon to exist elsewhere, whether the other country
is underdeveloped or developed. To attribute the majority of
our cultural characteristics to people of other cultures can only
result in a chain of misunderstandings and mistakes.

☐ **TWOFOLD JUDGMENTS**

The most hazardous tendency in the way of thinking that
Americans take with them into other cultural situations is that
of making twofold judgments based on principle. The struc-

ture of the Indo-European languages seems to foster this kind of categorization. Action in all situations is fostered by such judgments. An event or situation is assigned to a category believed high in value and thus a basis for positive action; or to one low in value and a basis for rejection, avoidance, or other negative action. Twofold judgments are the rule in American and Western life: moral-immoral, legal-illegal, right-wrong, success-failure, clean-dirty, modern-outmoded, civilized-primitive, developed-underdeveloped, practical-impractical, introvert-extrovert, secular-religous, Christian-pagan. The fact that such a method of dividing human activities into opposites is largely arbitrary is indicated by the necessity for Americans to compromise to solve problems. Compromising implies that neither side possesses "the truth" and that a just and proper solution can be achieved only by "splitting the difference."[79]

Judgment in terms of principle is very old and pervasive as a means of organizing thought in American and Western culture and is deeply rooted in the philosophy and religions of the West. It requires a very particular process and its special quality should be recognized. It is more than merely a habit of thinking in pairs. Other peoples have often invented dual ways of thinking: the Chinese Yin-and-Yang, the Zoroastrian dual (though equal) forces of good and evil, male and female principles, and forces of destruction and regeneration. However, other peoples do not usually rank one as superior and thus to be embraced on principle (the Christian God), while ranking the other as inferior and thus to be rejected on principle (the Christian Satan). Instead they will tend to rank the two categories as equal and say that each must have its due; or they may not connect them at all with principles guiding conduct.

In two of the world's largest religions, Buddhism and Hinduism, local beliefs which are quite distinct from those deriving from the theology of the dominant religion are permitted to live beside it. No one questions the fact that in Japan people may worship in a Buddhist temple and also in a Shinto shrine; or that they may observe the practices of Hinayana Buddhism in Laos and Thailand, while at the same time propitiating the "phi," the local non-Buddhist spirits. Actually, the normal religious practitioner in these countries has great difficulty in separating his Buddhist beliefs from his non-Buddhist ones. To him they all belong to the realm of the supernatural. This is quite different from the Christian attitude in which all that is supernatural, but not Christian, is superstition or paganism.

The average Western man, including the American, conducts his personal life and his maintenance of law and order in the community on principles of right and wrong, rather than on sanctions of shame, dishonor, ridicule, or horror of impropriety. He is forced to categorize his conduct in universal, impersonal terms. The "law is the law," and "right is right," regardless of other considerations.

☐   **WORK AND PLAY**

The habit of making twofold judgments based on principle is pervasive in American culture and is apt to distort interpretations of other ways of life. For instance, Americans maintain a twofold judgment of activity as either work or play. To most persons brought up in the present-day American environment of farming, business, or industry, work is what they do regularly, grimly, purposefully (for the money, or to do a good job, or to make a success) whether they enjoy it or not. It is a necessity, perhaps even more importantly, a duty, a "good thing in itself since one ought to keep occupied." A man is judged by his work. It is a serious adult business, for a man is supposed "to get ahead" or "make a contribution" to the community or mankind.

Play is different. It is fun, an outlet from work, without serious purpose except to make work more efficient. It is the lesser category and, though some of us may "enjoy our work," it is a matter of luck and by no means something that everyone can count on since all jobs contain some "dirty work," tedium, and tasks that one completes just by pushing on. Work and play are different worlds; there is a time and place for each; but, when it is time for work, then play and the lighter pursuits must be put aside.

The American habit of associating work with high purpose and grim effort, and play with frivolity and idleness (unless the play is considered as a therapeutic agent to do better work) is admirable at home, but it may be completely out of place in another culture. To insist on it, and to judge others negatively because they do not make the same distinction, can easily cause estrangement. In fact, for many peoples the times of most important work may also be the times of greatest festivity or highest ceremony. Work and play may be interwoven as thoroughly as two kinds of religious belief. A threshing floor may well be a dancing arena; building a new house or netting a school of fish may provide the occasion for a whole community to dance and sing together. Preparing the proper songs or dishes will be as "practical" an activity as the cutting of thatch or the care of the nets.

The combination of work and play is not a completely foreign idea to Americans, although urban, industrial society seems inimical to it. The American frontier, and even midwest farming communities until thirty and forty years ago, still combined the two in their husking bees, house-raising, and threshing parties. In the early part of this century, before wheat combines and farms of large acreage took over wheat threshing in midwestern states, farmers made the social and work rounds for several weeks in midsummer. Not only did they work together at these times; but they also feasted, socialized, and even managed a considerable amount of their courtships. It was a point of pride for each farmer's wife, with the help of the neighbor women, to have the largest and most elaborate quantities of food available for the men when they came in from the fields. The unmarried girls made a particular point of being there also, since most of the unmarried men were assembled. It was a gay time as well as a time of hard work.

☐ **TIME IS MONEY**

The way in which Americans distinguish between work and play can cause great difficulties in cultures. A good distinction of this sort is connected with American concepts of time. The more they are together, the sooner both foreigners and Americans become aware that their attitudes toward time vary. In many underdeveloped countries people speak of American time versus time of the country: *hora Americana—hora Mexicana,* or *mong Amelikan—mong Lao.* In general, American time is exact, people are punctual, activities are scheduled, and time is apportioned for separate activities.

Americans have frequent misunderstandings with the people of other nations because their attitude toward time is usually different, but nowhere is it more so than in relation to work. For Americans "time is money." Work is paid for in money and one balances his work against time or through regular periods for a set salary. Play or leisure time is before or after work time. An employer buys the time of his workers, schedules and assigns work as balanced against the time it will take, and budgets the wages against the time periods of his employees. Time can be turned into profit, for work turned out faster than planned can release extra time to do more work for extra gain.

The equating of work with time, using the least amount of time to produce the largest possible quantities, expecting that the time people are paid for be marked by sustained effort, and budgeting and planning man-hours in relation to cost of the end product are all central features of the American industrial economy and no small part of why it is so productive. Although they may complain about the necessity of routine and the tyranny of the clock in work, and even scheduled nonworking hours, Americans are thoroughly used to such strictures. Eating, sleeping, playing, recreation, even courting must take place during "time off." No wonder time is scarce and worth saving.

Such a concept of time is usually quite foreign to peoples of non-Western or non-industrial cultures. In most agrarian, peasant societies, work is not equated with time and scheduled solely in terms of production, but instead is geared to seasonal emergencies, climatic threats, or sporadic exhaustion of supplies and resources. Many routines reflect, not hourly or daily repetitions based on wage labor, but the crises of individual and social life, the cycles of the crops, the fluctuations in daily temperature, and the round of ceremonial observances. Thus, difficulties seem to arise when Americans or other Westerners try to get non-Westerners to accept their kind of scheduling and routine. Often trouble may start if Americans expect exact, regular attendance or steady, unflagging effort through fixed periods of times.

In Bolivia, where some mines run by Americans require a full eight-hour day, and others run by the French offer no better working conditions, and equal or less pay, many Indian miners prefer to work for the latter. This is because the French managers pay only for work performed and let the Indians go home when they please.[80] In Islamic lands, Friday is the Sabbath, but it is not a day of rest. Western archaeologists, who hired local Muslims to dig on their sites, often gave their workers the day off (without pay). This only made the Muslims bewildered and indignant. They wanted the money and their religious beliefs did not prohibit them from working on their Sabbath.[81]

In Trinidad, no problem arose when East Indian workers had industrial jobs with a high incentive (and relatively good pay). In order to keep good jobs in the refineries and offices of oil companies they were willing to adjust to the British schedules. On impermanent jobs of low pay, however, they were highly unreliable. Some were hired as coolies, particularly to mow the lawn in the compounds. At first, this work was paid for by hourly wages, but the administrators soon realized that workers would stretch a day's work to last a week in order to get the maximum amount of pay. The problem was solved by hiring them on a piece work basis, and paying a set sum of money for cutting the grass in a given area. Then there was no dallying.

As industrialism increases in the non-Western countries, and relatively well-paying jobs become available to workers, Western time scheduling will necessarily become more widely and easily accepted. In Mexico, where industry is growing rapidly, American type time scheduling has already made considerable inroads. Increasing employment in factories and office buildings is causing the spread of the quick lunch, eliminating both the siesta and the midday meal at home.[82] However, until industry and urbanism become much more important in these countries, traditional attitudes of time will prevail.

☐   **EFFORT AND OPTIMISM**

Another aspect of work that influences Americans in their conduct and decisions is that tied up in the words, effort and optimism. Effort is good in itself and with effort one can be optimistic about success. The high values connected with effort and activity pass quickly to the principle that, "It is better to do something than to sit back and do nothing." When there is an obstacle one should do something about it. Effort pays off with success. This thinking is based on the theory that the universe is mechanistic and man is its master and man is perfectible.[83] Thus, man can improve himself and control the part of the universe that is around him.

This national liking for effort and activity, and the optimism which holds that trying to do something about a condition or problem will almost invariably bring success in solving it, seems to be specifically American. Such attitudes are products of the continual expansion of culture during the past two hundred years, first along America's frontiers and later through its remarkable industrial growth. Obstacles exist to be overcome and bad conditions need only to be recognized in order to be rectified. Americans have confidence that, through effort, success will be achieved.

This traditional optimism of the American personality has been tempered to a certain extent in recent years because of international involvements, many of which present problems of a seriousness and complexity much greater than any faced previously. However, even if the optimism has been tempered (and perhaps realistically so), the method of overcoming obstacles has remained basically unchanged—put in a greater effort. If America has lagged in space achievements, or in the education of technical scientists, or in the development of successful international relations, the solution is to make a greater effort.

Effort and optimism also permeate the life of the individual American. Coming from an "open-class system" where status is usually achieved rather than inherited, both privilege and authority should be deserved and won. Effort, achievement, and success are woven throughout the fabric of American life and culture. Activist, pragmatist, and moralizing values rather than contemplative, theoretical, sensual, or mystical ones are integrated into the American character. Serious effort to achieve success is both a personal goal and an ethical imperative. The worthwhile man is the one who "gets results" and "gets ahead." A failure "gets nowhere," or "no results," for success is measured by results (though there is some "credit for trying"). The successful man "tackles a problem," "does something about it," and in the process "gets ahead." His success is measured in terms of his positive solution of the problem. A failure is unsuccessful through his own fault. Even if he had "bad breaks," he should have "tried again." A failure in life "didn't have the guts" to "make a go of it" and "put himself ahead."

This is a very severe moral code. We do not know how widespread it is among Americans, but it is recognizable to all of us. It indicates a culture in which effort is rewarded, competition enforced, and merit and personal achievement recognized. Unfortunately, the code raises problems that occur even at home. For instance, it calls all those in high positions successes and all those in low ones failures, even though we know that there is "a need for Indians as well as chiefs."

We have rounded up these clichés, not only because they are so characteristic of Americans, but also because they illustrate the activist spirit that permeates our foreign work efforts. The drive to do something about bad conditions and to achieve success in overcoming them is particularly American. Like other traits of culture, we cannot expect to find an identical one among peoples elsewhere, particularly in non-industrial countries; and, like all virtues, this one has its pitfalls and can induce cultural blindness.

This American habit of evaluating effort, optimism, and practicality in terms of results and success means that merit is the main justification for authority or high position. When we observe that those in authority elsewhere have achieved their position through other values, we may react by bewilderment, anger, or cynicism. If we decide that they are wrong and that we should do something about it, we are surrendering to a typically American, activist judgment. We then not only risk alienating the only individuals who could work efficiently with us, but we also risk diluting and misdirecting our efforts. This is because the obstacles with which we must contend are not found in cultural differences but in specific technical and institutional problems.

Another pitfall caused by such judgments is the possibility of shifting (usually unconsciously) from a high evaluation of work, which many peoples may share in their own fashion, to a need for busywork, hurrying, and pressuring; in short, to encourage a love of activity for its own sake. This is easy to do. There is already a tendency among the civil servants in many of the underdeveloped countries to concentrate on paper work, a legacy of their colonial days; so a reinforcement of this attitude by a belief that work for its own sake is good will not help the situation.

To peoples in other parts of the world, a history of failure in recent decades and centuries is as commonplace as the successes of America. Their experiences may well have taught them to value not effort and optimism but endurance, passivity, pessimism, acceptance, pliancy, and evasion. It is not because they have no interest in getting things done, but because they had so many reversals during the period when America was achieving its greatness, that they lack the confidence of Americans.

Before undertaking a project, they may make many preparations which to Americans may seem extraneous; such as extensive consulting with others and the building up of a consensus; giving favors to win personal loyalties; trying to conciliate the proposed plans with religious and traditional beliefs; and considering minutely all alternatives, including the realistic alternative of not risking action at all. American demands for bustle and effort, for getting down to business, may not only be interpreted as nagging, pushing, and ill-mannered; but sometimes may also be downright frightening, especially when a wrong judgment could lead to disaster. After an initial failure the American determination to "try again" or to "try harder next time" may seem particularly foolhardy. Merely to intensify effort and try again on a bigger scale when resources are limited may appear to them as the most reckless compounding of original folly.

Misunderstandings have frequently occurred in international committee rooms between Americans or other Anglo-Saxons and Latin Americans because of the Latin use of rhetorical speech in discussions. Americans want to "get down to business," to confine themselves to the agenda at hand and to eliminate the flowery talk to which the Latins are accustomed. The Latins oppose such pressure. Such directness is not the way they settle problems.

American assumptions about effort and optimism include an active response to the challenge of obstacles and bad conditions and also a faith in progress and a constant view toward the future. American hopes for its families and communities are built around the children and the generation to follow. There is an accent on youthfulness. The ideals, as exemplified by commercial advertising and entertainment, almost always emphasize the young, and the old are not generally honored or sought out despite their experience. In general, elderly people are bypassed, either left in "old folks" homes or in retirement, and in either case, removed ⌐ om the realm of practical life. This attitude differs greatly from that of non-Westerners, most of whom equate age with experience. The old are treated with deference and the oldest male is usually the arbiter of all family or community decisions.

American culture may be one of the few in which progress has long been a central value. This is because the American economy has progressed and expanded constantly ever since America emerged as an independent nation. In America, progress is equated with a better future, and with bigger and better successes; it also implies that the new and modern are explicitly better than the old and traditional. The experience of two world wars and the postwar international competition may have altered this view to a certain extent, but we still concentrate on the future and visualize it only as a better time than the present. Our technological and economic life must progress. No one expects it to be possible to keep America as it is today or as it was yesterday.

Americans should keep in mind that, for many peoples, their ages of glory were in the past, so the old ways are tried and true. Modernity and newness have no value in themselves for these peoples. Eventually they will change, because they know they must, but not because they feel life is constantly progressing.

☐ **MAN AND NATURE**

The greater effort that marks the American response to obstacles may seem shallow, irreverent, or undignified to peoples of other cultures. Some obstacles do deserve respect and there are limitations to what man can do, even if he is the cleverest animal that has appeared so far. The American attitude toward nature is a case in point. For many Americans the natural environment is something to overcome, to improve, or to tear down and rebuild in a better way. American man attempts to conquer nature, so he breaks the soil, harnesses natural resources, and divides plants and animals into categories of useful and harmful. Harmful or undesirable plants are weeds and undesirable animals are vermin—the first to be uprooted or poisoned and the second to be trapped, shot, or poisoned. A botanical definition of a weed is "a plant growing out of place," from man's point of view, of course. The same yardstick could be applied to the definition of vermin.

Many of the American man's achievements are in a large measure due to his conquering attitude toward nature. The highest agricultural productivity in the world is only one of such achievements. This farming record, however, was also due to the very large expanses of land available in America. Even so, the American has paid, and is continuing to pay, certain prices for his agricultural success. Natural resources, particularly forests and waters, have been squandered and despoiled over large areas. Nature's balance has often been upset; and some conservationists now believe that the powerful insecticides being used to control such "pests" as the Japanese beetle and Dutch elm disease are destroying as many useful insects and birds as harmful ones.

This conquering attitude toward nature appears to rest on two assumptions: that the universe is mechanistic and man is its master; and that man is a categorically different form of creature than all other forms of life. Specifically, they lack his unique attribute of a soul. In most of the non-Western world, nature is rarely conceived as being mechanistic and man is merely one form of life, different only in degree from the others. In most so-called animistic religions, all living creatures are believed to have something corresponding to a soul and there is no sharp dividing line between man, animals, and plants. Souls are even attributed to inanimate objects such as soil, rocks, mountains, and rivers. In the world of Hindus and Buddhists the belief in a cycle of rebirths strongly affirms man's kinship with nonhuman forms. In his endless cycle of life, a man can be an insect, an animal, another type of man, or a form of deity. Whether or not such beliefs are correct, many peoples' attitude toward nature is strongly influenced by them. Excluding Westerners, most people consider man and nature as one, and man works with nature rather than attempting to conquer it.

During long periods of trial and error, peoples of all cultures have worked out adaptations to their natural environment. Their adaptations may lack much by Western standards, but they do enable the inhabitants to get by, sometimes in quite difficult environments. Through experience, these peoples have evolved programs of conservation; methods of stretching and restoring their slim resources; and elaborate accommodations to climate, vegetation, and terrain. Some such adaptations, now embedded in tradition and religion, are: the Middle Eastern desert-derived patterns of Islamic ritual hygiene, austerity, and almsgiving; Japanese frugalities in house structure, farming, and woodworking technology; and Southeast Asian village economies in the measured use of rice, trees, and fish in the rainy lowlands. These and similar adaptations to natural environment are high developments in the balanced utilization of limited resources.

When, with a facile confidence that nature can be tamed by ever costlier, new mechanical devices, Americans or other Westerners attempt to brush aside the experience of centuries, it is perhaps exciting for the people being aided. However, they are not apt to be reassured if they have information concerning the realities of the environment that is ignored by the rushing, pushing, self-assured newcomers; particularly since the native solutions sometimes outlast the glamourous innovations. In environments that to us seem adverse, such as those of the rainy tropics, the arctics, or the desert, experience has shown that Western man's goods and machines do rot, rust, freeze, or grit up all too quickly, requiring huge and costly effort merely to keep them going. This is not surprising since our machinery has been developed primarily for use in a temperate zone where precipitation is spread more or less evenly throughout the year.

A graphic example of the lack of adaptability of Western machines occurred in recent years during the military struggles in Southeast Asia. Tanks and other mechanized land equipment were developed with the solid land of America and Europe in mind, but their use was drastically curtailed when the rice paddies of Vietnam and Laos became flooded. The mobile foot soldier, unencumbered with gear, could slip through the soggy fields and marshes and be constantly ready to fight, while the tank or halftrack was bogged down in mud. In 1960, a revolutionary faction in Laos merely waited until the rains had waterlogged the country to pull off a *coup d'état* in the capital. They were well aware that the main army forces, equipped with tanks and other American machinery, could not reach the city until the land dried up six months later. Whether or not dog teams are preferable to snow tractors in the arctic, or black goatskin tents to expensively treated fabrics under the desert sun remain moot points.

□   MATERIAL WELL-BEING

The rich resources of America and the extraordinary growth of its industry and economy, have brought about a wide-spread wealth of material goods and possessions such as the world has never before seen. Among our people there has been a wholesale creation and diffusion of the marvels of modern comfort: swift, pleasant transportation, a great variety of foods, central heating, instantaneous hot water and electricity, labor-saving household devices, and comfortable homes. We like such comforts and continue to gear our industries to produce larger quantities and better versions of them. We have assigned a high value, almost a "right," to comfort.

Associated with this attitude toward comfort, and due to the state of our medical knowledge, we have also come to regard cleanliness as a virtue. "Cleanliness is next to Godliness," we say, and uncleanliness usually has undesirable connotations or indicates low status. This does not mean that Americans have become "soft." In war and in overcoming obstacles or disaster we have proved our ability to face hardships. However, such times are only intermissions, endured in the belief that they will help us to re-establish the kind of life we value most, when our high standards of comfort and cleanliness will again prevail. In American civilization, such material well-being is both the criterion and the undeniable proof of success and progress.

Achievement and success are primarily measured in terms of material goods, both because they are abundant and because they are indicative of how much money an individual earns. Since there is little display value in the size of one's income or bank account, the average individual buys prestige articles that most people can readily observe: expensive clothing and furniture, fine cars, fancy houses and the endless variety of elaborate machinery with which they can be equipped—power mowers, barbecue paraphernalia, television and hi-fi sets, refrigerators, and dishwashing machines. A person's status is affected to a secondary extent by his level of education, type of occupation, and social behavior; but their value, too, is significant mainly in terms of how much income they help the individual obtain. For instance, a college professor who has earned his Ph.D. stands well below the status ranking of a business executive who may have no college education but who commands a much larger salary.

People other than Americans also value comfort and the saving of human labor but, not having been able to acquire as many labor-saving accessories as have Americans, they may have concentrated on the satisfactions of other needs. They may be more interested in achieving spiritual or esthetic goals than machines, which will shortly be outmoded anyway. Their choices are, of course, limited by their comparative poverty. Few other peoples have been able to have realistic hopes of obtaining all the varied devices that are available to the American. Therefore, comfort has not been so highly valued.

Given the opportunity, people of non-Western cultures may also turn to the satisfaction of their material wants. As they develop their productive capacity, this value will presumably grow with them. During the Mexican irrigation and road building program described previously, people tended to begin buying goods for their material well-being and comfort—better houses, new furniture, stoves, refrigerators, washing machines, air conditioners and motor vehicles. What they bought was dictated mainly by their financial position; that is, the wealthier people purchased more of the desired items; the poorer people less.[84] The demand for automobiles, better houses, and modern household devices is growing everywhere in the underdeveloped world. The emphasis on other values seems to outweigh those of material well-being and comfort only when the latter are unavailable, rather than being an indication of any basic preference for the less tangible values.

The world being as it is, divided roughly into have and have-not nations, there is one specific danger which the innovator may encounter. He will probably be quick to note the inferiority of comfort-producing mechanisms in the underdeveloped countries as compared to those to which he was accustomed at home. He may even tend to judge the host country by its possession or nonpossession of familiar conveniences, possibly punctuating his judgment by rude remarks about the state of the plumbing. He may have become so dependent on his native comforts as to spend a large share of his time and energy in achieving them or demanding them of his hosts.

There is no surer way to cut oneself off or gain the dislike of another people, particularly if they are poorer, than to insist ostentatiously and embarrassingly on the expensive luxuries of one's habitual way of life. Furthermore, to concentrate on creating an atmosphere of American comfort, a microcosm of American society and culture is thereby established, and it will tend to insulate itself from the local culture. It may be more convenient to buy all one's groceries in an American commissary. However, this means losing the opportunity to learn the buying patterns and dietary habits of the local people, a knowledge that could be partially learned by shopping at the local market. It may also be more convenient to travel in an American vehicle all the time; but this will eliminate the possibility of learning the bargaining procedures and transportation system of the local people.

In a study made in Trinidad, one of the authors usually travelled on the local jitneys along with a variety of Trinidadians. It turned out that the operation of such vehicles was quite a recent innovation, important economically as well as socially. A trip in one of these pirate taxis was a fine time and place to meet people and to gather information about the local culture. Total strangers, chatting with one another about local affairs, provided an excellent source of ethnographic information. There are many interesting and valuable experiences to be had in a non-Western culture, but material comfort is not apt to be one of them.

☐   **MORALIZING**

One of the most basic kinds of two-fold decisions Americans make is that of classifying actions and objects as good or bad. Whether discussing the conduct of foreign affairs or bringing up children, or any other action, it is generally agreed that Americans tend to moralize. While moralizing is one of the sources of America's great strength, it also creates pitfalls, particularly when it influences Americans in their relationships with other peoples.

Every people has its own code of morality as a part of its culture. A part of the inventory one must make to understand another people is the determination of the sort of judgments they habitually make about events, conduct and individuals. This can be difficult. We cannot assume that they will consider moral what we consider moral, or that their morals will be expressed as principles. Their moralities may rest on different bases from ours.

In many other cultures, rank or esteem, the dignity of a person, the honor of an individual, the compassion due an unfortunate, and the loyalty due a kinsman or co-religionist may all be important in moral judgments. Most forms of sexual behavior may not even be considered important in moral judgments; or where one sex (usually female) will be judged rigidly, the other will be judged very lightly. We are familiar with a morality based on the rule of law by a central government, and on a code of business and contract obligations of world commerce and industry. However, such concepts are new to most non-Western countries and often conflict with the old moralities.

The American habit of moralizing about behavior can lead to an even greater risk. It is more subtle and dangerous than mistaking a difference in moral standards as either amoral or "bad." It is the "cynicism" or "hard-boiled realism" acquired by Americans who over-react to the discovery that the model moral behavior they were taught to expect in parents, public servants, spouses, and other adults is not always present in real life. They react by becoming "tough," "cynical," and "wise" to the corruption of the world. Such reactions and recoil are dangerous because they encourage the cynic to believe that whatever varies from his version of the highest moral excellence is therefore of the lowest depravity. This view magnifies evil and turns what may merely be a difference in moral standards, or indifference to moralizing at all, into corruption. It leads an individual to seeing evil everywhere. The cynical moralizer who then goes on to action and decision may be pushing himself to wrong action that may be disastrous when working with another people.

An innovator should be particulaly wary of one particular reaction that may develop from a cynical attitude. It is the anger that comes from the belief that many foreign countries, particularly the under-developed ones, are more graft-ridden, corrupt, dishonest, and unprincipled than our own. If one learns that educated officials divert a part of the American aid into their own pockets; that the policemen, clerks, and lesser functionaries make extra charges for processing forms through their offices; that businessmen connive at tax evasion or deal in black markets; or that landlords exact extortionary rents; it is all too easy to play the cynic. It is then easy to conclude that in these nations graft is universal, privilege unchecked, corruption general, and the situation hopeless. However, rather than making a moral judgment, it is much better to learn which customs, privileges, laws, obligations, immunities, and standards of value really prevail.

For example, the same merchant who connives at customs evasion may honor a debt within his guild for which no contract exists. Customs payments are a part of the Western system of collecting money, not comparable to guild responsibilities which involve traditional honor. A tribal chieftain in the Middle East may instigate a cattle raid (where he still can) yet tribal custom may oblige him to give his life to defend a guest's goods. On the other hand, the police law prohibiting cattle raiding is not a firm tradition, but a part of the new nationalism. In Muslim countries, a policeman may pocket a minor present. However, he may give his life trying to arrest a thief, because the religious laws of Islam prohibit stealing. All people have loyalties and a sense of responsibility, but in many countries these qualities are not yet tied in with their allegiance to the laws of the nation. In other words, nationhood has not yet been fully integrated into their lives.

When we make strong moral judgments about corrupt officials in other countries, we should keep in mind that in our own country such moral judgments are backed up by rigorous penalties. An official caught dealing in graft will have to face severe prosecution and an elaborate system of law designed to punish him. If this penalty system was not in force here, it is doubtful, despite all our moral indignation, that graft could be kept within reasonable bounds. Even with strong legal deterrents, there are still too many individuals willing to take bribes and risk detection. Our penalty sytem developed along with our culture during the period of America's expansion. Most of the underdeveloped countries, however, are too young as independent nations to have yet elaborated similar systems. Where such systems do exist, they are still weak. Moreover, our codes of law and penalty, being largely based on European models, are for the most part foreign to their traditions. If the same weak penalties that prevail in the underdeveloped countries were the only legal deterrents in America, we might very well have even more graft and corruption than exists elsewhere..

☐   **EQUALITY OF MEN**

The moralizing tendency is interrelated with another important trait of American culture—egalitarianism. Social equality is actually more of a moral idea than a fact of our lives. Great differences of wealth, education, influence, opportunity, and privilege exist in the United States. Nevertheless, the experiences that Americans underwent along the frontiers and through the process of immigration did represent a huge historical experiment in social leveling. Our legal and institutional heritage prescribes equal rights and condemns special privileges, and demands equal opportunity and representation for every citizen. Our national manners, with few exceptions (such as the old-fasioned racial etiquette of the once slave-holding South), are standardized for nearly all adult citizens. It is said that we make a cult of the Average Man. Inequality—unless expressed through distinctions of achievement, merit, and worth—is wrong, bad, or "unfair." When inequalities, based on hereditary status or special privilege, result in arrogant manners, or in an extravagant juxtaposition of wealth and misery or of pomp and abject humility, the average American is shocked and uncomfortable. He will often push to remedy such situations.

Egalitarian ideals are all to the good and they have certainly proven so on the American scene. However, people other than Americans have long since contributed to the common fund of such humanitarian concepts. The Muslims have always taught that all men are equal under Allah, and racial intolerance has been at a minimum among them. The Arabs have never refrained from marrying people of other racial groups. Most feelings of superiority found in Muslim countries are mainly a matter of supposed relationships with their prophet, Mohammed.

However, the majority of the world's societies are hierarchically organized, show marked class and caste differences, possess distinct aristocracies, elites, and other privileged groups, and most importantly, accept such inequalities as normal. In general, sociologists and anthropologists believe that the differences between whites and Negroes in the United States are of a caste-like nature. However, this has not changed the basic American value judgment of equality among men. Open patterns of subordination, deference, and acceptance of underprivilege call forth humanitarian sympathies (American style) for the "underdog," and American values call for efforts to do something about such matters. This impulse to act tempts us, on our own moral grounds, to interfere directly in the way of life and the systems of values of peoples. To the American's patience, it is trying to have to deal with persons whose authority seems neither justified nor deserved, or to wait for the ordinary man who will act only when he has received the go-ahead from his figures of prestige or respect. Yet, with hierarchically organized people, the traditional approvals must be obtained.

One of the more recent forms of egalitarianism on the American scene is that of the comparative equality of the sexes. In practice, women are barred from the highest positions in our nation and are discriminated against in certain professions. However, their treatment is more nearly equated with that of males than in practically all non-Western nations. Most Americans consider marriage a kind of partnership, an unusual kind of marriage among the cultures of the world. This is a product of our liberal history and, at least insofar as the economy is concerned, it has proved beneficial.

Some social commentators feel that, despite its economic advantages, this concept of marriage has brought about other sorts of disabilities. In any event, it has not yet been proven that equality of the sexes is best for all peoples in all cultures. Furthermore, this kind of equality may prove to be irrelevant in developing more efficient technologies and institutions in other lands. People in other societies may have strong feelings about the status of women. Therefore, unless inequalities between the sexes are definitely limiting development or change, it is usually best to work within the prevailing system of values. If change does come in this sphere, it will have to come from the local people themselves.

American ideals of equality tend to create another difficulty. It is that of discerning local figures of aristocratic or prestige leadership when they do exist. If democratically-minded Americans find it hard to spot hierarchical patterns or organization, it is because too many of their own values and preconceptions stand in the way. For instance, that impoverished aristocrats or ascetic priests, beggarly in dress and looks, can still command respect and allegiance, despite their lack of outward signs of visible achievement and "success," is a difficult concept for Americans to grasp. Some people, like the Japanese, present another enigma; for they practice a kind of faceless leadership in which string-pullers exert their authority behind conspicuous but powerless puppet or ceremonial figures in public office.

A minor consequence of American egalitarianism is a preference for simple manners and for direct, informal, unpatronizing treatment of other persons. Americans are known for their informality and this can work to their genuine advantage if kept within limits. But, when abroad, a slavish adherence to simple, unaffected manners and forms of address can be disastrous. Especially in countries where people do differ in rank and prestige, American are likely to give offense if they are brusque, breezy and "kidding," treating all persons alike and impersonally. It is much better to try to acquire some of the local usages of long titles, flowery forms of address, language, and manners of courtesy and deference than to try to accustom foreigners to American ways. To neglect giving a man his due deference in countries where rank is important is to insult him. The American tendency of trying to make a foreigner into a regular or average guy by an informal, breezy, and "kidding" approach is dangerous. The informality of genuine kindness, courtesy, and unostentatious living is worth retaining. But when informality means belittling or disparaging a person whom his own society ranks high, then it is not advisable. American "kidding" and humor are very special products of an egalitarian culture. They are best kept at home.

In America, since all men are supposed to be potentially equal, and since success is an important individual goal, then a high value must be assigned to individuality. The characteristic is largely a heritage of our frontier days, when there was plenty of room and opportunity for the individual to achieve that of which he was capable. Due to the expansion of our industrial economy, and due to the increasing complexity and population of our society, individual action can no longer solve all problems. Cooperation is a necessity nowadays when large groups of people must work together. In the frontier days this was true to an extent, but the necessity became greater as the frontier became smaller and ultimately disappeared. Even then, because equality was a value, the manner of achieving individuality was not by accenting uniqueness but by stressing similarities. One might have more and better things than another, but they should be more or less the same kind of things. In this sense, even individuality evolved into a kind of conformity.

In America today, conformity has been emphasized even more by the necessity of living together in large groups, of accomplishing most of our aims through group effort (because it is more efficient). The organization man has superseded the rugged individualist. People are integrated into society through cooperation. Another indication of the weakening emphasis on individualistic action is the growing demand for security. There are only a few individuals who, through their own unaided efforts, are willing to risk an unknown future. Most Americans prefer to surround themselves with group insurances that cover all contingencies. In their efforts to attract new employees, employers advertise insurance benefits as much as the challenge of the work and the salary; and people buy insurance for the smallest items in their lives. Even household machines can be insured against breakdown. Government, too, becomes more and more involved in insuring the welfare of its citizens.

☐ **HUMANITARIANISM**

There is another value associated with egalitarianism that is also interrelated with our moralizing based on principles.

It is the widespread and justly famous American trait of humanitarianism, which so often expresses itself as generosity. Americans respond liberally to calls for help and give all they can to others when disaster strikes. The amount of efficiency they can display at such times is amazing.

A dramatic illustration of American competence during a tragic aftermath of a battle occurred recently in Laos just after the capital city, Vientiane, had been heavily damaged by military action. The American technical aid efforts in the years preceding had not been particularly impressive. They had been bogged down to a considerable extent by cultural problems with the Lao, as well as by administrative problems in the American organization itself. But when the capital was attacked and heavily damaged, and the population was in difficult straits, the American aid organization (International Cooperation Administration), as well as other American groups in the city, went into action in a manner that was truly remarkable. After the attack, the city was badly damaged; but within two or three weeks it was on its feet again, primarily due to American planning and work. The Americans thought nothing of working day and night at this task and their organizational ability was clearly demonstrated. In three or four months the marks of the battle were almost obliterated, all primarily due to American action in emergency.

American humanitarianism is certainly one of the finest heritages from our pioneer ancestors. The only possible pitfall in our manner of expressing this quality is that it is usually highly organized, institutional, and impersonal. For many other peoples humanitarianism is highly personal and sometimes entails taking into one's house and social life the recipient of generosity. The people of poorer countries do not usually share with everyone; they cannot. However, they do have their own patterns of sharing: through personal and kinship obligations, by religious almsgiving, and in other ways. The American pattern of impersonal generosity need cause no difficulty if we do not let it blind us to the existence of other patterns; if we remember that other peoples are just not as rich as we are; and if we do not turn our method of giving into a harsh standard of judgment against the peoples who lack it.

Let us take an example from the traditional land of beggars, *baksheesh,* and the outstretched palm—the Middle East. Here the halt, lame, and blind line up at the mosque or church door. The naive American reaction is likely to be condemnatory. "All these poor people! This community must be very cruel or backward not to take care of these people!"

A deeper look into the realities of Middle Eastern social and cultural organization shows that these beggars are, in fact, being taken care of by the community. Every member of the faithful in Islam gives ten percent of his income (the *zaka*) in direct alms to the unfortunates who personally ask for it. "Give a little and get a blessing in return." This particular pattern of generosity is one that has been worked into the communal life of the society, in keeping with its meager resources. Do not conclude that the people who support such a system are heartless and ungenerous, or assume that the beggars are making a good thing of it. The difference between this kind of generosity and the Community Chest is mainly one of organization and personalization.

7

FIELD
PROBLEMS

☐ **CERTAIN INSIGHTS**

The foreign innovator stands midway between his own culture and that of his hosts. His job is particularly complicated. He needs not only to understand something of the culture of the host country, but he should also be aware of his own cultural assumptions. This he must do without being a full-time social scientist. Moreover, he has his technical specialty, some part of which must be adapted to fit into the local culture—a burden that the social scientist does not have on his study trips abroad. The change agent cannot be expected to carry out a complete cultural study of the society where he is working. He can, however, obtain certain insights, all of which will prove invaluable. He can obtain this information through two channels: first, through the body of generalizations developed through anthropological and other social science research and case studies, and second, by means of his own observations, which can be facilitated by a guideline to field methods used by anthropologists.

Many social scientists feel that a fairly thorough study of a local culture ought to be made before deciding on and beginning a change project. However, at least in the near future, many if not most innovators will probably have to work without benefit of such studies. In such instances, the innovator should learn as much as he can from the written descriptions of the local culture in general, and as it applies

184

to his field in particular. Then he should seek as much additional information as he can find on his own.

Although the average change agent will not have the time, the desire, or the background training to devote to full-time research, he will have a considerable amount of spare time, and many opportunities for mixing with the local people. He will be able to move and live among them, unless he elects to go only to the houses and compounds of his fellow Americans. Unfortunately, the latter choice is made much too often, but it is self-defeating in the long run. Not only does it cut off the contacts that could provide information vital to the innovator, but it also cuts off the possibility of participating in and learning about a different and interesting kind of life—that of the host country. With few qualifications, the change agent is advised to take advantage of all reasonable cultural contacts with the people who are his hosts.

☐ **CULTURE SHOCK**

The first few days and weeks spent in a new country are as critical for the foreign change agent as they are for an anthropologist doing field research. This is the time when a visitor's attitude toward a country can be set positively or negatively. If, after passing through this period, the visitor has acquired a healthy attitude toward the local culture, he has won a big battle. It is natural for this initial period to be a disturbing one for a person from one culture suddenly confronted with the ways of another. Culture shock has been experienced by millions of people throughout history. It happens to tourists, tyro merchants, fledgling diplomats, bewildered immigrants, and social scientists, as well as to foreign change agents. Once an individual has adjusted to it, a cross-cultural situation can be the source of much inspiration and discovery. But the initial period is critical.

Some people have more tolerance and less anxiety than others when faced with new, unusual, or baffling situations. They may have had more exposure to cultural differences than others in their previous years. A varied environment in childhood, travel, learning another language well, are only a few of the kinds of experiences that can develop the tolerance and adaptability that build cultural bridges. But no one is a perfect chameleon. In nearly every prolonged contact that a person schooled in one culture has with that of another, some shock and forced readjustment occurs. It is compounded of frustration, exasperation, irritation, and the strain of heightened attention to strange cues and signs in a foreign situation.

A description of one such experience previously written by one of the authors will exemplify the problem:

"My first research trip in a foreign land was to India, where my intention was to make a study of urban factory workers. I made the initial contacts with the Indian members of the local university and seemed to be having no difficulties. A local schoolteacher was given the responsibility of taking me to a factory city, some fifty miles away from the university town, and finding me lodgings there. A room was located and I moved in.

"It was on the second floor of an apartment building on a narrow, dark street. On the street below there was a Hindu temple which I could see fairly well from my windows. Throughout the day Hindu worshippers came to the temple, rang a muffled gong, poured water on the *Shiva lingam* as an act of worship, and said Hindu prayers. Also, the chant of the Brahmin priests could often be heard. The temple floor was wet, shiny, and dirty from the spilled water and the innumerable bare feet of the people who came to worship. On occasion, cows would wander into the temple to eat the flowers left by the faithful. My room was a little dirty and there were mice in it.

"When I ventured outside, the people of the neighborhood stared at me as if I had come from Mars. Although there were Europeans and Americans in the city, they never ventured into this quarter. I had studied, and could speak, some Hindi but I was too shy to use it often; when I did, the local people seemed to have difficulty understanding me. Becoming more and more nervous in my surroundings, I decided to go to a nearby village where there were some workers who commuted to the city.

"Again the school teacher made arrangements for me and found a place in a relatively clean government guest house. There were no other guests, though there was an English-speaking Indian civil servant who lived just across the road and who was willing to serve as an interpreter. I obtained a temporary servant from a nearby village.

"My next task was to start interviewing the village people, but I was too shy and kept postponing the inevitable. I could talk enough with the servant to send him to the market for some tea and a few edibles. The servant did as he was told except for several details he misunderstood. When he returned from the market he prepared tea. The room was barren of furniture except for a table and a couple of chairs. When I reached for some sugar, which was in a paper bag just as it had been purchased, I found it crawling with ants. I took sugar anyway, picking out the ants, and instructed the servant to put it out of reach of the insects.

"I drank my tea in a state of nervous tension because the servant squatted just in front of the table and watched my every movement as if I had two heads. I wanted desperately to be alone, but was not sure I could explain this properly to the servant without hurting his feelings. After all, the servant was from the village where I wanted to do my research. Ultimately the servant went away, to my relief, but when he had gone I found the bag of sugar on the other chair and a veritable convoy of ants travelling to and fro, carrying off the sugar. The sight of these ants and my inability to handle what should have been a simple situation were very irritating.

"When evening fell I was upset by the many unfamiliar sounds coming from the nearby village and the surrounding countryside. All the bird calls were unfamiliar and there was constant yapping from what I later learned were jackals. I slept very fitfully that night. When morning came I was so upset by the unfamiliarity of everything that I went out and caught the first train to the city. I returned to my family in the university town without even bidding my host goodbye.

"However, I did come back to the scene of my trials after several days, and stayed for a year to complete my research work. Most of what had been unfamiliar and frightening in this first week became understandable and not unpleasant after I became accustomed to my new surroundings. I learned to move freely, both through the industrial city and the nearby villages, and to use my Hindi tolerably well with the local people."

This example of culture shock is probably sharper than most overseas workers will experience, since they are not expected to live in as intimate association with the local people as is an anthropologist. Moreover, they are not so much on their own. There is normally a fairly large American organization which helps take care of their needs and acts as a buffer between them and the local community. Nevertheless, they will be affected by the strange culture to some degree and, since they will not have received the orientation of a social scientist, the cultural differences will be more unexpected.

The simplest manifestation of culture shock is a ludicrous tendency to raise one's voice to a shout when one finds a foreigner unable to understand simple English. At its strongest, culture shock can have various effects: it can reduce one to numb fatigue (as in early attempts to follow a foreign language), to anger against the foreigners confronting one, or to a frenzied retreat into the familiar. One anthropologist defines the symptoms as "excessive preoccupation with drinking water, food, and dishes; fear of physical contact with servants; great concern over minor pains and skin eruptions; a hand-washing complex; fits of anger over delays and other minor frustrations; a fixed idea that 'people' are cheating you; delay and outright refusal to learn the language of the country; an absent-minded-faraway-stare (sometimes called the tropical stare); a feeling of helplessness and a desire for the company of people of one's own nationality; and a terrible longing to be back home, to be able to have a good cup of coffee and a piece of apple pie, to walk into that corner drugstore, to visit one's relatives, and in general, to talk to people who really make sense."[85]

When and if such a reaction occurs, it is important that the innovator recognize it for what it is—a temporary attitude that will pass as soon as he becomes familiar enough with the local customs and manners that at least some of them will be predictable. The only cure for culture shock is a forced-draft, purposeful pushing-on ahead. The way to get over it is to work at making new persons and new ways familiar and known, to return to them again and again until the strangeness is gone.

Such a solution is well suited to American activist values. Brooding about the situation certainly will not improve it. The real danger is that, at this early stage, the change agent will reject the local culture as inexplicable, then turn to his fellow countrymen, and to familiar activities, as being the only sensible ones.

We have treated this phenomenon as one that occurs during the initial stage of an innovator's stay in a new country. Although problems of adaptation may continue to arise throughout this tour, the most difficult period is at the beginning. The change agent will continually have to learn new ways and adjust to them; and, as more and more of the culture is understood, the easier it will be to accept new forms of behavior in stride. Surprisingly enough, culture shock will reoccur each time an individual encounters an unfamiliar non-Western culture. However the shock may be less severe on the second and subsequent occasions.

☐ RAPPORT

The change agent, just like the anthropologist or other social scientist, must win some degree of acceptance and confidence for himself within the community, institution, or group where he will work. He must gain the support of the local people at least to the extent that they will talk with him freely and sincerely about the real conditions and interests of their lives. Such rapport is a must before any work that requires the voluntary consent or cooperation of the local people can begin. The more speculative social and psychological sciences, as well as the more practical disciplines such as medicine, psychiatry, and education, agree in stressing the importance of good rapport between the investigator and his subject.

In the field of the social sciences, an investigator should not find rapport hard to establish if he displays a genuine interest in a people and a desire to understand them. People will respond to inquiry concerning their lives more easily than might be supposed. There is probably no subject which an individual finds more interesting than himself, including his beliefs and behavior. Secondarily, he is interested in his neighbor, and the combination of self and enough neighbors constitutes the human element of a culture. Added to the natural desire of people to talk about themselves, the sincere, interested Westerner has a definite advantage simply because he is a Westerner who is interested. In the past, most Westerners were uninterested in the customs of non-Western people or had an initial negative bias. To meet Westerners who are interested in their culture for the purpose of learning rather than of criticism is an experience few non-Westerners can resist.

There are certain precautions innovators should observe in order to gain the minimal confidence essential for their work. The ways of winning rapport can be as varied as cultures. No single method can be relied upon. However, there are some general guidelines that can be followed. When making acquaintances with some people, typically American tactics may be successful; with others, American manners may be so strange as to be misunderstood or even to appear downright offensive. Thus, back-slapping, or "kidding around," or a casual invitation to "make yourself at home, we're always informal," may be as unfathomable to another people as Japanese hissing (a sign of politeness), German stiff bowing, or Latin-American *abrazo* (mutual embracing) are at first to Anglo-Americans.

In general, it is best to act with reserve until one is fairly familiar with native patterns of interaction. If, after a while, one finds that the local people act with informality, American customs can then fit in easily and nothing will be lost; but if their behavior is highly formal, then it will probably never be wise to act in an American way. To foster rapport does not imply converting others to American ways; but rather responding to the cues they give, being aware of some of the values they hold, and making some adjustment to their culture. This does not mean to ape them indiscriminately; it means rather to follow their lead in matters important to them.

Because of the variety of customs and manners which are found in different cultures, the general rules for winning rapport can be stated in the simplest terms. Nevertheless, they add up to an honesty and directness of approach which is worth spelling out.

1. Explain truthfully but as simply as possible your purpose in asking for and accumulating knowledge about the local culture. Your inquiry may be suspect at first, but people are flattered by genuine queries from respected strangers. If nothing happens that suggests hidden motives, their suspicions will fall away and they will have no option but to accept the fact that none are present. A lie or false pose will soon be apparent and it will damage the investigator's reputation for integrity.

2. Proceed to new subjects or enter new places for purposes of observation only with the consent of the people involved, and if possible by their request or invitation. Secret observation too closely resembles spying. The innovator interested in a local culture has neither the rights nor duties of a cross-examiner, nor the privileges of a priest, doctor, or lawyer. What is sacred or dangerous in their beliefs may not be discussed openly; whereas that about which they are proud will be volubly discussed.

3. Respect native values, conventions, taboos, and prejudices, even if you cannot go along with all of them. Ignorance of local mores may be forgiven, but not contempt or wanton disregard for them.. If you ask for guidance, you will not only learn native customs but show your good faith to your hosts.

4. Maintain confidences. Information given to you in confidence must not be indiscriminately disclosed, certainly not

if it may prove harmful to the informant. Social scientists have always tried to keep their informants anonymous.

5. Refrain from making moral, esthetic, or other judgments about the culture or the persons from whom you are learning. Where your purpose is to find out what you can, any condemnation of the source of information or judgment on the information itself is not only irrelevant, but is likely to estrange your informant or to distort your own understanding. Some reactions of surprise, incredulity, or disdain are involuntary and unavoidable in cross-cultural contacts. Remember that what you consider superstition is merely a kind of belief that is not substantiated by your beliefs. The good investigator of another way of life is like a good diplomat. He keeps a poker face and finds a way to turn a compliment in any situation. A continual display of one's immediate reactions is not only naive; it is a sure way to close off further and deeper contact with persons of other cultures.

6. Avoid expressing nostalgia, chauvinism, vainglory, or making invidious comparisons between your own culture and the local one. You are not in a debating society. If your purpose is to build rapport and get information, it does nothing but harm when, even unintentionally, you disparage the ways of other people. If your informants want factual information about your own way of life (and many will), give it to them honestly. There is an enormous curiosity about American life; and the change agent, whether he likes it or not, will be both observed and listened to as a "typical" American.

7. Come acceptably vouched for, work from the top down, and try to stay clear of too close identification with any level or faction. The innovator, like the anthropological field worker, ultimately depends on community acceptance and his objectivity. The research field worker has it a little easier in this respect, for he is in the community only to know and understand the way of life. The innovator has a more difficult role because he is in the community to bring change. But the local people will also notice whether or not he is genuinely interested in the local culture for its own sake. It is a com-

mon experience in social science that you get the best results and most information if you follow the lines of personal relationship; if you descend a hierarchy gradually; and, if when you work with a fairly low-ranking person, you have at least seen, though not necessarily committed yourself to, higher authority or prestige. To work from the top down is to pay the necessary deference to the scale of values the community holds. Some lines of relationship unite all levels and most factions in any culture. One must find them and follow them, and yet stay clear of close identification with any of them.

These rules from social science research experience for winning and holding rapport may appear very stern. But experience has taught that useful information about people comes only through careful diplomacy. One should have a genuine respect for the persons from whom one is learning. Foreign innovators, as well as social science workers, should keep in mind that their subjects are human beings who can and will veil and distort vital information unless they are treated with the proper tact and consideration.

☐ **PARTICIPATION IN LOCAL CULTURE**

Although direct questioning can produce a certain amount of information, anthropologists have found that studies based only on spoken statements are incomplete. This is because people don't always do what they say they do. Every culture has its morals and ideals. When people are questioned directly about what they do, they tend to express the ideal pattern of behavior, or else to tell the questioner what they think will please him.

For instance, in village India one might inquire as to the occupations of the Brahmins and Chamars. The answer might be that the Brahmins were priests and the Chamars leather-workers. Yet, investigation might show that both Brahmins and Chamars in a particular village were primarily farmers. The

Brahmins would know how to conduct certain ceremonies, and would do so in their spare time; but their main economic support would come from the cultivation of their fields. The Chamars would be the traditional tanners of leather; but they would have given up this occupation in order to eliminate the stigma of unclean work. They too would depend on farming for their livelihood. In Trinidad, when one of the authors noticed that many rum shops were operated by East Indians, he asked several local people if Muslims ever operated them or drank rum. He received a negative response in keeping with strictures of Islam, which forbid the drinking of alcoholic beverages. But investigation showed that many of the Muslims drank rum, and that some operated rum shops. Other Muslims then explained that such people were not good and that things were not as they had been in the old days.

In these cases the actual culture differed from the verbal one. Anthropology distinguishes between these cultures by terming them the *real* and the *ideal*, and both kinds are found almost everywhere. This is because people tend to pay lip homage to their moral code long after they have ceased conforming to it. The significance of this is that one cannot rely completely on what people say, even when they are trying to be sincere. The only way around this difficulty is to observe what people do.

Another disadvantage in getting only verbal information is that much which might be significant to the questioner is not brought up in conversation. The informant takes most of his own life and culture for granted and, not knowing what might be significant to the questioner, neglects to mention many small details and even fairly large incidents. In Laos where there is a considerable variety of spirit beliefs, one of the authors collected verbal statements about many of the spirits from a local Lao. Most of the stories were about spirits that had bothered people far out in the remote villages and were told as if they had happened long ago. Then one day the author saw a man standing rigidly in the town market place, his hair dirty and dishevelled, and his clothes in rags. The merchants were throwing him scraps of raw meat. The author's informant quite willingly told him that the man was possessed by a tiger spirit and had been around town for sometime. It had not occurred to the informant that the author would be interested in this person.

Cultural participation has another real advantage. One of the best ways of convincing the local people that one is interested in their way of life is to seek their help in learning their ceremonial and social customs. Most people of the non-Western nations think that Westerners look down on their religious and social beliefs and practices. They are not unjustified in this attitude because most Westerners who were overseas before these nations achieved their independence did feel superior and usually took no pains to hide the fact. Though political conditions have changed, some of the old attitudes still persist.

A change agent can gain no end of good will and rapport by letting the local people know that he would like to attend some of their religious ceremonies, weddings, funerals (in Buddhist countries funerals are not a time of sadness), and other communal activities. At first they may be a little surprised and not quite sure he is serious; but given a little encouragement they will make every effort to include him in their gatherings. If he shows genuine interest, even participating when possible, the local people will be greatly pleased. In all but the most conservative cultures he will soon be swamped with invitations to attend local affairs. His hosts will explain with great patience what the ceremony means and why they do what they do, and he will learn much. He will also build up a kind of confidence that is difficult to gain merely by asking people what they do without observing their behavior.

A final advantage of this type of participation is that the innovator will develop new interests during his overseas tour. The recreational facilities open to a Westerner in the underdeveloped countries are far inferior to those back home. He may, therefore, have considerable time on his hands if he restricts himself only to his work and his customary pastimes. If he can open the gate to the exotic culture of the people with whom he is living and can develop a genuine desire to learn their ways, he will find new interest in both his work and his leisure. A true cross-cultural experience is of great value in enriching the personality of the twentieth-century man. An American or any other Westerner should retain a continuity with his own culture in an overseas situation. Nevertheless, an anthropologist would feel that he was missing many unique opportunities if he spent all his free time with American colleagues playing poker, going to parties, and attending American movies.

For gathering information on the local culture, observation and participation are as necessary as verbal data; and there is no better method of establishing good relations and rapport than by taking part in local activity.

☐   **THE LOCAL LANGUAGE**

A change agent's work is always made easier if he can use the native language. Conversing in the local idiom will make much more knowledge available and decrease the possibility of misunderstandings. However, adequate comprehension and fluency in a language are not easily acquired. It means spending much time studying; and, in view of other responsibilities, this time is not always available.

Experience indicates that any foreign language can be learned by anyone of normal intelligence. In the plural societies of Asia and Africa, people consistently learn one another's languages; sometimes individuals with little or no formal training learn as many as four or five. They do not study the other languages formally, but merely imitate the speech of their neighbors over a period of months or years. However, they are living right in the cultural milieu where the language is spoken. This situation is not often duplicated for most foreign specialists who spend much of their time among their fellow countrymen. Even the advantage of formal training will not eliminate the need for considerable conversational interchange before achieving proficiency in the new language.

In general, even when a change agent receives basic groundwork in a foreign language, he will not achieve fluency or anything approaching it, unless he starts speaking it regularly when he arrives at his post. Many Americans get interpreters as soon as they arrive at their posts because they want to get on with their work quickly. Then, as their responsibilities increase, they find they have less and less time to devote to language study; and, with the interpreter available, they make less and less effort to speak the language themselves. The availability of an interpreter is certainly a stultifying influence in learning another language. If one really intends to converse in a language, there is really no way of avoiding the uncomfortable initial period of bumbling through.

Earlier, we noted that American missionaries invariably learn the language of their area and sometimes more than one. They, too, usually study formally at first. However, as soon as they arrive at their posts, they deliberately throw themselves into situations where they must speak the local language—and always without the presence of an interpreter. In South Asia it was a common practice for Protestant missionaries to spend three to six months living in a villager's house where no English-speaking person was available. Admittedly, this is a pretty strong dose of cultural saturation, but it is one way of learning the language and much of the culture of a people. When these American guests had completed their stay with the villagers, they could get along comfortably, if not with complete fluency.

Many foreign specialists are not expected to go through a similar experience; but, if they want to speak the local language intelligibly, they should spend a fair amount of time actually conversing, and without the assistance of an interpreter. Even if a person never achieves fluency, any simple phrases he can learn will be useful in terms of rapport. Many people of the non-Western nations have concluded that Westerners consider their language, as well as much of the rest of their culture, inadequate. So any indication from a Westerner that he does not feel this way, even though he does not speak the language fluently, will help to alter this unfortunate concept. Using the local idiom is an important way of participating in a people's culture.

Many change agents depend on interpreters for their working relationships. Therefore, a careful choice of interpreter is extremely important. Just because an individual speaks good English and seems to know the local language well is not enough. He can be a bridge or a wall. People coming from another nation or culture, who are called third nationals, are quite often hired as interpreters simply because they sometimes speak English better than do the local interpreters. The disadvantage of such persons is that they may feel superior to the local people or may not be accepted by them. They may be from cities in their own countries and have little knowledge of villagers' needs. The result will be that, however worthy the innovator's intentions, communication between him and those he is trying to help will be filtered through the prism of the relationship existing between his interpreter and the local people. In short, a local interpreter is better than one from the outside.

Of course, the change agent ought to be sure that the interpreter really knows the local language well. He should watch to make sure that the interpreter is not hiding a gap in his knowledge of the local language by telling the innovator what he thinks people mean. Finally, he should instruct the interpreter to translate the words of informants fully, that is, give their equivalents in English literally. The interpreter should not summarize or choose what he thinks is important for the innovator to know. That should be left to the innovator.

☐   **FIELD PROCEDURES**

The change agent, like the social scientist, needs to decide what is representative or typical in the local situation before gathering data for his projected innovation. He needs to be able to make some estimate as to how general his findings will be. He needs to do some sampling by going out to see a variety of situations. He needs to know what village type is most "typical," what combination of distinct religious or ethnic elements are most often found together and in what regions, and what the consistent problems are in most villages of a region or the whole country. Without some such rough sampling he cannot expect to be able to apply findings in one region to the problems of another.

Once the problems of rapport are under control and the innovator decides where is he going to work, he faces the problem of deciding from whom he will get his information. The anthropologist uses native informants, depending on them for explanations of their way of life, and working with them systematically. This does not mean that he asks them in so many words: What are your beliefs or customs? He does not even ask them to describe categories of culture that seem significant to a Westerner, such as religion or social relations or technology. Such subdivisions of human activity may be unfamiliar to them unless they are already Westernized to a considerable extent.

The anthropologist's approach is to seek detailed facts about local customs, step by step, going through the ramifications of each custom as it comes up. If he wants to learn about the local patterns of family life and kinship, he systematically and in the local language goes through the names of all the personal relatives of the informant. He then collects anecdotes about real life incidents that show the interrelationships of all members of the family. The researcher must make the generalizations; he cannot expect the informant to do so. He cannot ask the informant if age is a determining principle in status position. Rather he himself must decide this on the bases of how young men greet their fathers and uncles, who keeps the money in the family, and what happens to a person when he gets beyond his active years. Most people take their own culture so much for granted that they are unable to analyze it.

Native, local informants are best precisely because they are not sophisticated generalizers. They describe the local situation concretely and either they are unable or are not tempted to gloss it over, pretty it up, distort it, or disguise it in the interest of theory and pseudo-systematics. For the same reason, a learned informant can be unreliable, not because he knows less (though he probably will be less directly in touch with real village conditions), but because he pre-digests the information. In this sense he can be as much a barrier as can a bad interpreter. He passes the information through a sieve of theory or evaluation that distorts it for the inquirer, the more so because the inquirer cannot be certain of the informant's set of values. Later the questioner may be able to see what was untrue, but in the beginning he must take most of the information at face value. He is on surer grounds if he gets it directly from an unsophisticated citizen.

Gathering information by directly questioning simple people about real life is one of the chief contributions anthropology has made to social science methods. Direct questioning may be taxing, time-consuming and perplexing at first. However, consulting experts relying entirely on written sources is not good enough. There is no royal road leading down to the "grass roots." Where the scholarly expert occupies a class in society far above the cultivator or artisan, as in most non-Western nations, or where a well-educated elite is found, it is plausible to believe: "If you want to learn about farming or iron-working, why talk to the (ignorant) village farmer or smith? Talk rather to the distinguished professor of agriculture or metallurgy." But we can counter that social science has progressed almost to the point at which inquiry has been pushed to the man at the grass roots level.

The field methods that have been described are based primarily on anthropological research. Since the anthropologist is concerned with description only, he tries to achieve a fairly complete coverage. On the other hand, although the innovator can put to good use all the information that he personally elicits, he will not, under most circumstances, have the time, nor perhaps the interest, to do as thorough a job as the anthropologist. But even if he limits his research to his own technical specialty—education, agriculture, animal husbandry, or village administration—the same field methods should be used.

The anthropological field worker takes cultural inventories. Confronted with an unfamiliar culture, he must act both as an explorer and a collector. The innovator must do likewise, but in a much more limited manner. He should at least ascertain the real limits of resources and conditions available to the people of the area where he is working. The anthropologist draws up a catalogue of everything worth noting that distinguishes a culture—tools, implements, furniture, homes, clothing, plants, medicinal supplies, foodstuff and the method of its preparation, ritual objects, songs, legends. All are grist for his mill. He wants to be able to identify the items of his research in the native language and to understand how and in what way they are used. Other classifications of his research may answer questions as to the social or ancestral derivation of an item, its possible connections with myth or legend, whether it is communally or privately owned, how it is inherited, whether or not it is used in religious offerings, whether it is obtained by trade or through ties of kinship, and so on endlessly.

The innovator may not be able to make such a complete survey, but he can try to get such information as concerns his project. Even narrowed down to his specialty, such research may prove to be a complex undertaking, because of the interrelatedness of customs in the local culture. That is, agricultural practices often involve religious beliefs, and are also affected by such intangibles as social relations, food preferences, and trade practices.

A stranger may not at first understand enough of the intricate web of interconnections, nor command enough of the language, to follow native descriptions and explanations of the culture. Nevertheless, in most groups some persons can usually be found who are ready and able to impart this sort of information to a newcomer. Patient and systematic work with such individuals has no substitute. It is the real secret of anthropological field work, the reason why anthropologists seem to be able to grasp the innermost meanings of a new culture faster than others. Similarly, linguists have learned that, to get an unbiased description of the local language, they must avoid the professional grammarian and seek the simple native who is innocent of scholastic sophistication and preconceptions. In the same manner, the anthropologist learns best when, with a native informant, he moves patiently and systematically, from object to object, and from subject to subject.

The innovator will not have full time to devote to research of this sort. A really well-informed local consultant can provide valuable information. In addition, by maintaining a lively curiosity concerning the new and unknown life around him, and even through casual questioning, he may detect cultural connections of vital concern to his job.

Anthropologists have found it essential to take regular and extensive notes regarding their cultural findings. It is particularly important to take them at the start of a project before adapting oneself too much to the local way of life. The differences in customs, sights, and sounds will be very apparent in the first few weeks and months. Later, many such cultural differences will have become a part of one's accepted way of life and therefore hardly noticed. Anyone who takes notes will notice that the incentive to write them, hence the quantity of them, will decrease as time goes by. However, if a good understanding is to be had, one should continue to take them throughout the whole period of one's stay. Most anthropologists make a rule to write some notes every day, for the amount of knowledge desirable concerning culture is almost limitless. The fact that one has learned to get along comfortably in another culture does not mean there is not much more to be learned. Even in our own culture, which most of us have experienced for the greater part of our lives, there are enormous areas of activity of which we may be unaware or of which we lack understanding.

Whether one takes notes in the presence of the informant or writes them down later, in privacy, will depend on the general personality type of the inhabitants and the relationship of the informants to the innovator. If people are suspicious of an outsider's motives, note-taking can put them on edge and either make them reluctant to continue talking or cause them deliberately to distort the facts for some supposed advantage. On the other hand, if they understand why the interrogator is taking the notes and are in sympathy with his aims, note-taking may not bother them at all. Anthropologists have found that certain peoples are so interested in having their culture described and preserved in writing that they are more willing to give information if it is written down in their presence. Whether or not to do this should be decided on the basis of a people's reaction; in general it is best to start by writing notes after an interview or after one has gathered some information. With a little practice, considerable detail can be remembered.

Whatever the amount of research on the culture, it can be divided into three phases; pre-study, on-going analysis, and evaluation. These phases of research are also necessary in connection with the actual innovation; but here we are concerned only with cultural influences. Most anthropologists feel that a fairly thorough study of the whole culture of a people should be made before plans for change are set into motion. However, such a study is a fairly specialized job that most change agents are not prepared to undertake. Moreover, there is usually a time factor that prevents the individual from devoting himself full time over a fairly prolonged period to a study of the whole culture. The next best recourse for the innovator is to familiarize himself with the culture as much as possible through written sources; then to conduct as much of an informal survey as possible.

A change agent may not be able to make a thorough analysis of the whole culture, but he should try to achieve an understanding of the relationship of his own specialty to the culture with all its ramifications. If agricultural practices have ties with religion and social organization, he should also have some understanding of these, particularly of the aspects that affect farming. His plans should be projected with all the significant aspects of the culture in mind. Then, once his program is under way he should keep checking the cultural problems that arise as a result of the innovation. This is the time when blockages or unforeseen consequences may appear because of cultural interrelationships. As we have already noted, wells may not be tended because the village headmen, who were charged with their maintenance, do not have the authority to direct the chores of the villagers. The compost pits may not be used because handling household wastes is woman's work; and the women, with a strong standard of modesty, will not go to the pits at the edge of the village to deposit the wastes. When cultural factors such as these are learned, a project can be adjusted to fit the new knowledge.

Finally, it is to be hoped that every change agent will be interested in making an evaluation both of what happened to his particular innovation, and of what happened to the culture as a result of its acceptance or rejection. Such case studies of successes and failures are of great value in making wiser decisions in the future.

Appendix

by Arthur H. Niehoff

☐   **A Selected List of Case Histories of Socioeconomic Change Projects**[*]

The case histories listed in the following are efforts to induce changes in the practices of societies in the developing nations. Although almost all have basically economic ends, they include efforts to improve conditions in health, agriculture, education, home economics, cooperatives, transportation, and community development. Most of them concern efforts to assist rural villagers in Latin America, Africa, the Middle East, and Asia. They can be used by the student or teacher who wishes to go deeper into the problems of inducing change. Seventeen, marked by asterisks, have been reprinted in *A Casebook of Social Change,* edited by Arthur H. Niehoff.

Ablett, R. N. "Community Development in the Former Somaliland Protectorate," *Corona* (London, April 1961), pp. 138–41. To promote community development activities centered on halting soil erosion caused by bad grazing methods and the indiscriminate cutting of trees in one district, July 1958–60 (Somalia).

Adams, Richard N. "A Nutritional Research Program in Guatemala," in Benjamin D. Paul, ed., *Health, Culture and Community.* New York: Russell Sage Foundation, 1955. To carry on nutritional experiments involving supplementary feeding for school children in a small farming village (Guatemala).

[*] Adapted with permission from "A Selected Bibliography of Cross-Cultural Change Projects," by Arthur H. Niehoff and J. Charnel Anderson, Human Resources Research Office, George Washington University.

Aggarwala, C. M. "Nagwan: A Study of Self Help," *Kurukshetra* (Delhi, India, November 1952), pp. 10–12, 18. To promote a wide variety of community development projects in a single rural village of 800, 1947–52 (India).

"Akowonjo Village Poultry Improvement Scheme," *Community Development Bulletin* (London, September 1951), pp. 78–79. To introduce a new breed of poultry and encourage new feeding and housing methods in a rural village of 256, October 1949–December 1950 (Nigeria).

Alers-Montalvo, M. "Cultural Change in a Costa Rican Village," *Human Organization*, 15:3–5 (Ithaca, New York, Winter 1957). Two projects: to introduce an insecticide to combat pests and to intensify cultivation of home vegetable gardens in order to help correct vitamin deficiencies in the local diet in a village of approximately 340 small landowners (Costa Rica).

Allen, H. B. *Rural Reconstruction in Action*. Ithaca, New York: Cornell University Press, 1953. Primarily to influence agricultural practices in crops and animal husbandry in five peasant villages, but eventually to involve well drilling, malaria eradication, and literacy programs in a 35-village area (Iran, pp. 1–27); to influence home economic and hygiene practices in small rural communities (Syria, pp. 50–60); to organize sociocultural activities (mainly recreation) in two rural villages of 2,000 and 1,200 respectively (Lebanon, pp. 65–73); to establish a national public school system when none had existed for two years (Eritrea, pp. 91–95).

American Friends Service Committee. *A Village Development Project in Jordan*. Philadelphia, 1958. To reintroduce grape cultivation into a five-village rural area of 3,500 population, 1953–56 (Jordan, pp. 42, 88, Appendix E-3); to introduce new breeds and upgrade poultry quality in a rural five-village area of 3,500 population, 1954–56 (Jordan, pp. 53, 87, 93–94, Appendix E-7).

° American Friends Service Committee. "The Tur'an Agricultural Project," *Community Development Bulletin* (London, September 1956), pp. 79–85. To improve the agricultural practices of an Arab village of 1,600 near Nazareth by introducing the use of modern agricultural machinery, fertilizer, and new practices in order to help integrate them into the economy, March 1950–May 1955 (Israel).

Amoako, J. B. "Registration of the Physically Handicapped Persons in the Upper Region," *Advance*. Ghana Department of Social Welfare and Community Development (October 1961), pp. 57–61. To conduct a five-month campaign in the Upper Region of Ghana to register handicapped persons so the government could formulate a program to help them (Ghana).

Andrews, Stanley. *Technical Assistance Case Reports*. Washington, D.C.: International Cooperation Administration, 1960. To build a series of dikes on the sides of hills to catch runoff water and, by seepage, irrigate pastures, 1952–54 (Jordan, pp. 19–22); to set up a series of government-sponsored storage houses in various parts of the country to gather grain in fruitful years to use in lean years, 1954–60 (Jordan, pp. 28–30); to introduce improved varieties of wheat seeds and set up seed treatment stations to combat wheat diseases, 1952–60 (Jordan, pp. 30–31); to develop and implement a program to eliminate salting of the land in the Indus River Valley, 1952–54 (Pakistan, pp. 57–60); to introduce a systematic garbage collection and disposal service to reduce the health hazard in Amman, the capital city, 1951–60 (Jordan, pp. 67–70); to set up a public health testing laboratory to serve the country, 1951–60 (Jordan, pp. 68–71); to drill 3,000 tube wells for irrigation purposes in the states of Punjab, Pepsu, Uttar Pradesh, and Behar, and at the same time to train Indian personnel in the techniques of well drilling, 1951–58 (India, pp. 73–82); to conduct a malaria eradication campaign for the entire country, 1951–60 (Thailand, pp. 95–98, 102–03); to conduct a campaign aimed at controlling water and filth-borne diseases (mainly through building wells and privies) at a village level: 1957–60 to cover 52 villages in a pilot project, 1960–62 to cover 500 villages, next twenty years to cover all 40,000 villages (Thailand, pp. 98–104).

Askwith, T. G. "Some Community Development Schemes," *Progress Through Self-Help*. Nairobi, Kenya: The Eagle Press, 1960. To initiate a limited number of community development projects (constructing cattle pens and outside kitchens, digging latrines, and erosion control) in a village complex within one valley, 1958–59 (Kenya, pp. 14–17); to initiate a wide variety of community development projects in one district of Kenya, 1957–59 (pp. 22–26).

Barnett, H. G. *Anthropology in Administration*. Evanston, Illinois: Row, Peterson, 1956, pp. 143–50. To create community pride and awareness by organizing a community center for recreation and intellectual activities, 1952–53 (U.S. Trust Territories).

° Berelson, Bernard, and Freedman, Ronald. "A Study in Fertility Control," *Scientific American* (New York, May 1964), pp. 29–37. To initiate a family planning program into an urban district of Taiwan.

Buck, Pearl. *Tell the People: Mass Education in China*. New York: American Council, Institute of Pacific Relations, IPR Pamphlet No. 16, 1945. Originally to promote literacy instruction, but eventually spreading out to agriculture, public health, and community development projects, in a northern county of China of 472 villages with a population of 400,000, 1924–45 (China).

Cabreros Laya, Juan. *Little Democracies of Bataan*. Manilla: Inang Wika Publishing Co., 1951, pp. 93–108. To initiate community improvement projects in one neighborhood of a Philippine town, 1950–51 (Philippines).

Carpenter, A. J. "A Mass Literacy Campaign in South-Eastern Nigeria in the Autumn of 1949," *Mass Education Bulletin* (London, September 1950), pp. 73–79. To conduct an adult literacy campaign in a district of southeast Nigeria covering 500 square miles and a population of 80,000 adults, April 1949–January 1950 (Nigeria).

Carr, D. E. B. "Adult Literacy in Buganda," *Corona* (London, April 1952), pp. 144–48. To conduct literacy campaigns based on the Laubach method in the province of Buganda, population 1,296,240, 1948–51 (Uganda).

Cassel, John. "A Comprehensive Health Program Among South African Zulus," in Benjamin D. Paul, ed., *Health, Culture and Community*. New York: Russell Sage Foundation, 1955. To introduce changes in the diet and thus improve nutrition in a community of 16,000 Zulu tribesmen (South Africa, pp. 22–25); to introduce eggs and increase milk consumption for nutritional purposes in the diet of a community of 16,000 Zulu tribesmen (South Africa, pp. 26–29); to overcome the resistance to treatment of pulmonary tuberculosis in a community of 16,000 Zulu tribesmen, and to begin combatting this disease (South Africa, pp. 29–34).

Castillo, Hernan; Castillo, Teresa; and Revilla, Arcenio. "Accopata: The Reluctant Recipient of Technological Change." Ithaca, New York: *Human Organization* monograph, 1963. To initiate an irrigation system in a highland Indian community (Peru).

Chadwick, E. R. "Fundamental Education in Udi Division," *Fundamental Education* (Paris: Unesco, October 1949), pp. 9–21; and "Communal Development in Udi Division," *Oversea Education*, (London, January 1948), pp. 627–44). To promote a wide variety of community development projects in a single division of Onitsha Province, Nigeria, with a population of 300,000, August 1942–48 (Nigeria).

Christian, H. L. "The La Plaine 3-F Campaign," *Community Development Bulletin* (London, December 1953), pp. 20–22. To induce the 1,500 inhabitants of a village to improve their nutrition through a 3-F campaign (Food for Family Fitness) based on growing vegetables, improving poultry and other small stock, and general home improvement, 1948–52 (Dominica, West Indies).

Cohen, Ronald. "The Success That Failed, An Experiment in Culture Change in Africa," *Anthropologica* (Ottawa, Canada, Vol. III, No. 1, 1961). To convince the farmers to use phosphate fertilizers in a small district capital of 2,000, June 1956–March 1957 (Nigeria).

Compere, Gilberte, and Pierand, Alphonsine. "An Experiment in Rural Community Development," *Community Development Bulletin* (London, June 1962), pp. 81–85. To persuade local farmers living on two large hills to cultivate coffee on plantations already in existence as a cash crop through cooperative methods, one year (Rwanda).

° Cooper, B. K. "New Eruwa," *Corona* (London, June 1952), pp. 225–27. To establish a model planned village and induce people to move from the old village, which was unhealthy, overcrowded (population 8,000), and located on worn-out land, a 3-year project (Nigeria).

Cottrell-Dormer, W. "Community Development in the South Pacific," *Mass Education Bulletin* (London, September 1950), pp. 71–72. To help one rural village set up and operate a rice mill (New Guinea).

Court, John W. "The Adult Literacy Campaign in Northern Nigeria," *Oversea Education* (London, July 1958), pp. 64–68. To conduct a literacy campaign in northern Nigeria, 1946–58 (Nigeria).

Coutts, Philip. "Five Dams: A Community Development Project in Uganda," *Corona* (London, August 1953). To build five dams

through voluntary labor in a single county of 60,000, January–
August 1952 (Uganda).

Covar, Prospero. *The Masagana/Margate System of Planting Rice: A
Study of an Agricultural Innovation.* Quezon City: Community
Development Research Council, University of the Philippines, 1960.
To introduce a new system (the Masagana/Margate) of planting
rice and improved seeds into twelve barrios of one district, 1954–58
(Philippines).

Cowper, Lawrence T. "Rural Health Education," *Community Development Bulletin* (London, March 1958), pp. 26–29. To conduct a
pilot sanitation and health education program centered on rodent
control in a rural village of 1,000 (U.S. Trust Territories).

Cowper, Lawrence T., *et al.* "Village Sanitation Campaigns on Guam,"
South Pacific Bulletin (Noumea, New Caledonia, October 1958).
To conduct a sanitation campaign in a rural village of 1,000, several
weeks (U.S. Trust Territories).

* Dobyns, H. F.; Monge, Carlos; and Vasquez, M. C. "A Contagious
Experiment," *Saturday Review* (New York, November 3, 1962),
pp. 59–62. To promote community development projects centered
around agriculture, health, and education on a hacienda (Vicos)
of 35,000–40,000 acres and 380 families (1,800 people), 1952–57
(Peru).

Donkor, S. S. "Sandema Builds a Post Office," *Advance.* Ghana Department of Social Welfare and Community Development (October
1961), pp. 61–64. To build a post office in a single town, which
served as the district seat, by using communal labor, a few days
(Ghana).

Dowling, M. A. C. "Mauritius: The Malaria Eradication Scheme,"
Corona (London, December 1950), pp. 452–56. To conduct a
malaria campaign that would eliminate malaria from the island
population of 450,000, 1948–50 (Mauritius).

Dube, S. C. *India's Changing Villages—Human Factors in Community
Development.* Ithaca, New York: Cornell University Press, 1958.

Einseidel, Luz A. *Success and Failure in Selected Community Development Projects in Batangas.* Quezon City: Community Development
Research Council, University of the Philippines, 1960. To upgrade
the quality of locally raised swine in a barrio of 1,174 people by
bringing in new breeds, December 1957–June 1958 (pp. 34–38);
to immunize the cows, carabaos, and horses (about 100 animals)
in one village (pp. 38–41); to introduce new and improved swine
into a village of 525 (pp. 41–43); to introduce new and improved
breeds of swine in a village of 586 (pp. 43–47); to induce the
spraying of fruit trees in a village of 1,000 (pp. 47–51); to promote
chemical spraying to combat plant pests in rice, mangoes, etc., in
a village of 533 (pp. 51–53); to stimulate the people in a village
of 646 to construct a footbridge across a nearby river (pp. 54–56);
to construct a footbridge for a village of 1,020 that was practically
an island (pp. 56–60); to help a village improve a six-mile road
to a nearby municipality (pp. 60–62); to help a barrio of 700 build
a bridge across a ravine to one of its sitios, a smaller unit of the

barrio—this one has a cluster of 10 houses (pp. 63–65); to build a community center in a village of 620 (pp. 68–70); to build a community center in a barrio of 410 (pp. 70–74); to construct a community toilet in a barrio of 1,865 (pp. 74–77); to construct a health center in one village, using self-help techniques (pp. 77–79); to build a community toilet in a barrio of 172 households (pp. 80–82).

Erasmus, C. J. *Man Takes Control*. Minneapolis: University of Minnesota Press, 1961. To introduce soil erosion control methods into a southern district of Chile, 1952–55 (pp. 17–21); to carry out a yaws eradication campaign in northern coastal Ecuador and the Pacific coast of Colombia, 1950–52 (pp. 26–27); to reduce the incidence of infectious diseases by installing a pure water supply in an Andean community in Ecuador and to operate a charity maternity hospital for lower-class mothers in Quito, 1951–52 (pp. 27–31).

° Evans, A. J. "The Ila VD Campaign," *The Rhodes-Livingstone Journal* (Capetown, South Africa, No. 9, 1950), pp. 40–47. To conduct a venereal disease campaign among the 10,000 members of the Ba-Ila tribe, September 1946–50 (Zambia).

"Everybody's Uncle," *Maryknoll* (June 1959), pp. 20–24. To organize a credit union among the poorer inhabitants of Puno, whose population is 16,000, 1955–59 (Peru).

Faulkner, D. E. "A Pilot Scheme of Village Betterment in Lagos Colony, Nigeria," *Oversea Education* (London, July 1951), pp. 152–59. To enlist the help of the local people in building "village institutes" in six rural villages of 500–6,000 people each, these institutes in turn housing welfare teams that promoted community development projects, December 1947–51 (Nigeria).

da Fonseca, Wanda Gomes. "An Experiment in Community Development in a Suburban Community in Brazil," *Community Development Bulletin* (London, December 1961), pp. 25–28. To promote a variety of community development projects, based on self-help, in a suburb of a city in northeast Brazil.

° Fraser, T. M. "Sociocultural Parameters in Directed Change," *Human Organization* (Ithaca, New York, Spring 1963). To introduce protected water supplies and sanitary latrines to a rural complex of 67 villages with a total population of 60,000 (India, pp. 96–98); to introduce improved stock and upbreed the quality of local poultry in a rural complex of 67 villages with a total population of 60,000, 1952–60 (India pp. 98–100); to establish a cooperative for leather workers and weavers in a rural complex of 67 villages with a total population of 60,000, several years (India, pp. 100–02).

Goldsen, Rose K., and Ralis, Max. *Factors Related to Acceptance of Innovations in Bang Chan, Thailand*. Ithaca, New York: Cornell University, Department of Far Eastern Studies, Southeast Asia Program, No. 25, 1957, pp. 30–37. To encourage the use of modern health facilities in a rural hamlet complex of 1,600 (Thailand).

Hanks, L. M., Jr., and Hanks, Jane R., *et al.* "Diphtheria Immunization in a Thai Community," in Benjamin D. Paul, ed., *Health, Culture and Community*. New York: Russell Sage Foundation, 1955. To alert a rural community of 1,700 to the dangers of a possible diphtheria epidemic and to cause their children to be assembled for inoculation (Thailand).

Hastie, P. "Women's Clubs in Uganda," *Mass Education Bulletin* (London, December 1950), pp. 4–6. To promote work among the women in one district of southern Uganda by establishing clubs where cooking, sewing, child welfare, and some academic subjects were taught, and entertainment was organized, 1946–50 (Uganda).

Hay, Hope. "Mass Literacy in Northern Rhodesia," *Quarterly Bulletin of Fundamental Education* (Paris: Unesco, July 1949), pp. 11–17. To conduct an intensive mass literacy experiment at a mine compound of 3,692 (2,437 being totally illiterate) by using Laubach's individual teaching method, January 1945–December 1946 (Zambia).

Hayden, Howard. "Community Development in Moturiki, Fiji," *Oversea Education* (London, January 1953), pp. 2–12. To conduct a pilot project in which a native team, trained in Fiji, would use the self-help technique to promote a wide variety of community development projects (agriculture, health, education, etc.) on a single island of 527 persons living in nine villages, February 1950–December 1951 (Fiji).

Holding, Mary. "Adult Literacy Experiment in Kenya," *Oversea Education* (London, October 1945), pp. 204–08. To conduct a literacy campaign among women in one district, 1942–44 (Kenya).

Holmberg, Allen R. "Changing Community Attitudes and Values in Peru: A Case Study in Guided Change," in Richard N. Adams, ed., *Social Change in Latin America Today*. New York: Random House, 1960. To promote community development projects centered around agriculture, health, and education on a hacienda (Vicos) of 35,000–40,000 acres and 380 families (1,800 people), 1952–57 (Peru).

Holmberg, Allen R. "The Wells That Failed," in Edward H. Spicer, ed., *Human Problems in Technological Change*. New York: Russell Sage Foundation, 1952. To drill six wells to furnish a stable water supply for irrigation and sanitation purposes in a valley community of 2,000 (Peru).

Honigmann, J. K. "A Case Study of Community Development in Pakistan," *Economic Development and Cultural Change* (Chicago, April 1960), pp. 288–303. To develop self-help and self-planning in a rural village of 2,000, 1956–58 (Pakistan).

Hsu, Francis L. K. "A Cholera Epidemic in a Chinese Town," in Benjamin D. Paul, ed., *Health, Culture and Community*. New York: Russell Sage Foundation, 1955. To utilize Western medical facilities and practices to combat a cholera epidemic in a rural Chinese market town of 8,000 (China).

Jordan, P. "War on a Worm," *Corona* (London, October 1957), pp. 369–72. To conduct a campaign to eliminate the parasite causing elephantiasis on a six-mile-long island of 4,000 people in Lake Victoria (Uganda).

* Junod, Violaine. "Entokosweri: Managing a Community Service in an Urban African Area," *Human Organization* (Ithaca, New York, Spring 1964), pp. 28–35. To set up a family welfare center for health and home education purposes in a township of 60,000–80,000 for the use of 120–130 families in a four-block area, 1946–49 (South Africa).

* Khan, Akhter, and Moksen, A. K. M. "Mobilizing Village Leadership," *International Development Review* (Washington, D.C., September 1962), pp. 4–9. To carry out 24 drainage and irrigation projects, mainly reclaiming existing canals, in a single county of 100 square miles (Pakistan).

Khan, Anwarzzaman. *Introduction of Tractors in a Subsistence Farm Economy.* Comilla, East Pakistan: Academy for Rural Development, Nazeria Press, 1962. To introduce tractors to replace bullocks in a village complex of one state, 1959–62 (Pakistan).

King, Clarence. *Working With People in Small Communities.* New York: Harper and Brothers, 1958. To rebuild a road through a small rural village, fall 1953–spring 1954 (Mexico, pp. 26–32); to carry out integrated projects in transportation education, public health, and cooperatives in a rural village of 1,200 (Nigeria, pp. 77–92); to establish adult education and recreational activities, aimed at fostering a community spirit and training future development leaders, 1951–52 (Cook Islands, pp. 93–102); to build a milk station in a small rural community, April 1951–September 1952 (Puerto Rico, pp. 115–28).

* Lear, John. "Reaching the Heart of South America," *Saturday Review* (New York, November 3, 1962), pp. 59–62. To promote community development projects centered around agriculture, health, and education on a hacienda (Vicos) of 35,000–40,000 acres and 380 families (1,800 people), 1952–57 (Peru).

Lewis, Oscar. "Medicine and Politics in a Mexican Village," in Benjamin D. Paul, ed., *Health, Culture and Community.* New York: Russell Sage Foundation, 1955. To establish a cooperative medical clinic in a rural village of 3,50 (Mexico).

* Link, Eugene P., and Mehta, Sushila. *Victories in the Villages—India,* Plattsburgh: New York State University College, mimeographed, 1964.

* McDonald, J. C., and Keen, K. "The Kaifong Welfare Associations," *Community Development Bulletin* (London, December 1955), pp. 2–9. To organize welfare organizations built around a spirit of mutual self-help among the residents of the Shamsuipo District, population 100,000, 1949–55 (Hong Kong).

McGairl, J. L. "Urban Community Development Through Adult Literacy," *Community Development Bulletin* (London, September 1953), pp. 71–77. To promote an adult literacy campaign in the municipality of Dar-es-Salaam, aimed especially at reaching the periphery or shanty villages on the edge of the city, 1952–53 (Tanzania).

MacLean, Una. "Blood Donors for Ibadan," *Community Development Bulletin* (London, March 1960), pp. 26–31. To conduct a blood donor campaign and organize a blood bank in Ibadan, April 1957–October 1958 (Nigeria).

* Mahony, Frank. "Report on a Study of the Pilot Project in Range Management Near Afmadei," *Community Development Review*

(Washington, D.C., June 1961), pp. 34–39. To introduce pilot range management into a 30- by 32-mile area by building 11 vars (water catches) and limiting the number of people and animals using the area in order to get maximum range benefit (Somalia).

Mason, H. "Progress in Pare," *Oversea Education* (London, July 1952), pp. 9–14; and *Corona* (London, June 1952), pp. 212–19. To begin with a literacy campaign, then to expand into community development projects (especially soil erosion control), in the Wapare tribe of 20,000 people, 1949–51 (Tanzania).

Mayer, Albert. *Pilot Project India.* Berkeley: University of California Press, 1959. To build and improve roads in a rural village complex (pp. 166–69); to introduce improved seed varieties to a rural village complex, 1948–54 (pp. 239–48); to introduce new agricultural implements and tools into a rural village complex, 1948–56 (pp. 248–54); to introduce improved animal husbandry techniques in feeding, breeding, inoculation, and housing to a rural village complex, 1949–56 (pp. 255–59); to reclaim eroded lands along rivers through village self-help projects, 1949–55 (pp. 259–62); to establish cooperative brick kiln industries in a rural village complex, 1948–54 (pp. 272–77).

° Mehta, Sushila. *Working with Village People.* New Delhi: National Fundamental Education Centre, 1965. A collection of twelve case histories of efforts to promote community development in villages (India).

Meier, Gitta. "El Embalse: The Creation of a Community Through Community Organization and Urban Renewal," *Community Development Review* (Washington, D.C., June 1960), pp. 18–47. To test the feasibility of self-help techniques in improving or rebuilding one's own dwelling among 103 families in a five-block slum area of San Juan, two years (Puerto Rico).

Millard, I. S. "The Village Schoolmaster as Community Development Leader," *Mass Education Bulletin* (London, June 1950), pp. 42–45. To introduce the growing of tomatoes as a cash crop into a small district (two square miles) of 2,000 population, 1935–49 (Jamaica).

° Miner, Horace. "Culture Change Under Pressure: A Hausa Case," *Human Organization* (Ithaca, New York, Fall 1960), pp. 164–67. To convince the Hausa tribes in Northern Nigeria to keep the brush cut along streams and destroy the habitat of the tsetse fly, 1937–47 (Nigeria).

Mtawali, C. W. "A Health Campaign in Tanganyika Territory," *Community Development Bulletin* (London, June 1951), pp. 54–56. To conduct a pilot health campaign aimed at eradicating venereal disease from a single chiefdom of 10,000 people, 1949–50 (Tanzania).

Najafi, Najmeh. *Reveille for a Persian Village.* New York: Harper and Row, 1958. To initiate a community development program centered around health and education in a rural mountain village, 1955–56 (Iran).

° Nicholl, Robert. "Pilot Literacy Scheme in the Ulu Paku, Sarawak," *Oversea Education* (London, July 1951), pp. 141–52. To conduct a literacy campaign in rural Sarawak, based on the Laubach method, among ten long-houses holding an average of thirteen households each, December 1949–August 1950 (Sarawak).

° Niehoff, Arthur H. "Theravada Buddhism: A Vehicle for Technical Change," *Human Organization* (Ithaca, New York, Vol. 23, No. 2, Summer 1964), pp. 108–12. To provide driven and dug wells in a number of villages in 1958–61 (Laos).

Niment, Don. "A Nyeri Youth Club," *Community Development Bulletin* (London, December 1959), pp. 2–4. To build six "youth clubs" where unemployed young people would receive instruction in literacy, agriculture, and homecraft, and to provide for sports and social functions in one district (Kenya).

"No More Crop Lifting," *Kurukshetra* (Delhi, India, October 1955), pp. 131–35. To construct a water tank (catchment) and provide badly needed irrigation water for a rural village, 1953–54 (India); to build a catchment tank and provide irrigation water for a rural area, 1954–55 (India).

Norris, Thomas L. "Decision-Making Activity Sequence in a Hacienda Community," *Human Organization* (Ithaca, New York, Fall 1953), pp. 29–30. To induce the 200 families of a large hacienda to build sanitary outhouses, winter 1950–51 (Costa Rica).

O'Dea, Thomas F. "Changing Attitudes Toward Economic Cooperation," *Community Development Review* (Washington, D.C., March 1958), p. 48–52. To counter the effects of a potato blight by introducing blight-resistant seeds, fertilizer, and insecticides to a hacienda of 35,000 acres inhabited by 2,000 Indians, 1952–55 (Peru).

° Orata, Pedro T. "Community Education in Rural Philippines," *Oversea Education* (London, April 1954). To put an end to damage done by loose animals through the building of pens and promoting the enforcement of ordinances against offenders in a single rural village (Philippines, pp. 5–7); to build a feeder road to the main provincial road for service to 68 families in a rural village (Philippines, pp. 12–14).

Orata, Pedro T. "A Philippine Village Experiment," *Fundamental Education* (Paris: Unesco, October 1951), pp. 105–11. To initiate a variety of community development projects in a small rural village of 471 households, 5 weeks (Philippines).

Padmore, H. J. "Adult Education in Grenada," *Oversea Education* (London, October 1946), pp. 401–03. To conduct an experimental adult education campaign (literacy and social activities) by setting up schools in the seven largest towns in 1945–46 in Grenada (West Indies`.

Palmer, J. E. S. "Self-Help to Irrigation," *Community Development Bulletin* (London, March 1962), pp. 44–45. To carry out a small irrigation scheme near a single rural village, and to test the reaction of the people to irrigation and dry season work, 1959–61 (Nigeria).

Pelep, S. "Ponape Fishermen Set Up Successful Cooperative," *South Pacific Bulletin* (Noumea, New Caledonia, October 1960), pp. 48–49. To promote a fishing cooperative among approximately 100 island fishermen, May 1959–October 1960 (U.S. Trust Territories).

Philips, Jane. "The Hookworm Campaign in Ceylon," in Howard M. Teaf, Jr., and Peter G. Franck, eds., *Hands Across Frontiers*. Ithaca, New York: Cornell University Press, 1955. To introduce mass hookworm treatment in rural Ceylon, 1916–20.

Poston, R. W. *Democracy Speaks Many Tongues*. New York: Harper and Row, 1962, pp. 1–14. To organize, establish, and maintain institutions for the blind (Guatemala).

Purseglove, J. W. "Community Development on the Uganda-Congo Border," *Mass Education Bulletin* (London, June 1950), pp. 46–50. To move 20,000 people out of an overpopulated area and establish them in a new one, and to permit the practice of crop rotation on both the old and new land, 1944–49 (Uganda).

Richardson, F. L. W., Jr. "Everyone Who's Hungry Can Belong to My Church," *Human Organization* (Ithaca, New York, June 1943), pp. 44–48. To induce the natives in a rural village complex to move from their worn-out highland patches to virgin bottomland, 1925–38 (Angola).

Roberts, Lydia J. *The Doña Elena Project*. Rio Piedras, Puerto Rico: University of Puerto Rico, Department of Home Economics, 1963.

° Schweng, L. D. "An Indian Community Development Project in Bolivia," *Community Development Review* (Washington, D.C., March 1963), pp. 13–19. To oversee land reform procedures on an estate of 500 families and to follow up with an integrated community development program, 1954–56 (Bolivia).

Seegers, Scott, and Seegers, Kathlean. "Colombia's Extraordinary Teacher-Builder," *Reader's Digest* (Pleasantville, New York, March 1963), pp. 111–15. To promote the building of schools in rural communities in one state of Colombia, 1920's to date (Colombia).

Shamsudeen, A. N. "Lessons From a Set-Back," *Oversea Education* (London, July 1956), pp. 60–61. To promote a fundamental public health education campaign by printing up a series of simple pamphlets for mass distribution at popular prices (Pakistan).

° Sibley, W. E. "Social Structure and Planned Change; A Case Study From the Philippines," *Human Organization* (Ithaca, New York, Winter 1960), pp. 209–11. To initiate a variety of village improvement programs in a rural community of 400 (Philippines).

Singh, Rudra Datt. "The Village Level: An Introduction of Green Manuring in Rural India," in Edward H. Spicer, ed., *Human Problems in Technological Change*. New York: Russell Sage Foundation, 1952. To introduce the practice of "green manuring" (plowing under of plants for fertilizer) to increase land fertility in one district (India).

Smith, E. W. "Adult Literacy in Western Uganda," *Oversea Education* (London, April 1957), pp. 25–29. To conduct short, six-month literacy campaigns in Western Uganda.

Smith, E. W. "Kenya: A Community Development Project," *Corona* (London, July 1952), pp. 267–68. To organize literacy classes in one district of Kenya where the people were 90 per cent illiterate, 1950–52.

Smith, William C. "Hens That Laid Golden Eggs," in Gove Hambidge, ed., *Dynamics of Development*. New York: Praeger, 1964. To introduce an improved variety of chickens into a rural community (Mexico).

South Pacific Commission. *The Koror Community Center*. Noumea, New Caledonia, Technical Paper No. 46, August 1953. To organize a community center in the capital city of Koror (populated by 2,000 Palauans), the program being built around recreation, education, discussion groups, and so forth, 1952–53 (U.S. Trust Territories).

Stycos, J. Mayone. "Birth Control Clinics in Crowded Puerto Rico," in Benjamin D. Paul, ed., *Health, Culture and Community*. New York: Russell Sage Foundation, 1955. To reduce birth rates through a nationwide population control program dispensing birth control information and devices (Puerto Rico).

Tannous, Afif. "Positive Role of the Social Scientist in the Point Four Program," in Lyle W. Shannon, ed., *Underdeveloped Areas*. New York: Harper and Row, 1957, pp. 334–36. To install a sanitary water supply in a small rural community of a few hundred (Lebanon).

Taylor, P. J. O. "The Community Schools: Zaria Province, Northern Nigeria," *Community Development Bulletin* (London, September 1954), pp. 79–81. To promote self-help school building projects in a province of 800,000, where the government could not furnish enough schools to fill the demand. A plan was developed whereby villagers built their own schools with government advice, and the government furnished the teachers, 1952–54 (Nigeria).

Unesco. Division of Community Education. *Community Education in Puerto Rico* (Occasional Papers in Education No. 14), pp. 12–18. Paris: Unesco, 1952. To establish a communal vegetable garden on unused land belonging to the school in a barrio of fifty families, June 1950–October 1951; to build a bridge across a river separating a barrio from a nearby town, December 1950–July 1951; to repair and paint a schoolroom and build an annex to it to serve as a kitchen and warehouse, in a barrio of 132 school children, October 1950–October 1951; to rebuild a public bathhouse in a barrio of one hundred families, June–July 1951.

University of Virginia. Extension Division. *Experimenting with a New Crop* (Bulletin No. 142). Charlottesville, Virginia (April 1953), pp. 1–6. To introduce the cultivation of rice into three villages in the Northern Territories of the country, 1952–53 (Ghana).

Uzoma, R. I. "Adult Literacy Work at Akriba in the Delta of the Niger," *Oversea Education* (London, July 1948), pp. 737–41. To conduct a literacy campaign among 10,000 members of the Okrika clan of the Ijaw tribe in coastal Nigeria, September 1944–February 1946.

Wainwright, Bridget. "I Was a Homecraft Officer," *Corona* (London, August 1954), pp. 297–98. To organize women's clubs in the local villages within a 50-mile area and to teach cooking, sewing, child care, hygiene, 1951–53 (Kenya).

Wainwright, R. E. "Women's Clubs in the Central Nyanza District of Kenya," *Community Development Bulletin* (London, September 1953), pp. 77–80. To organize women's clubs and spread knowledge of homecrafts among the rural women of a district of 500,000 population, 1951–53 (Kenya).

Wellin, Edward. "Water Boiling in a Peruvian Town," in Benjamin D. Paul, ed., *Health, Culture and Community*. New York: Russell Sage Foundation, 1955. To induce housewives in a rural community of 200 families to boil water before using or drinking it (Peru).

Yao Darko, Charles. "The Story of Nkwabeng Water Supply," *Advance*. Ghana Department of Social Welfare and Community Development (January 1962), pp. 69-71. To improve the water supply in a village of 3,000 by cutting the brush and cementing the spring, two years (Ghana).

REFERENCES CITED

1. Fraser 1963, pp. 96-98
2. Wagley 1952, pp. 4-5
3. Shannon 1957, pp. 2-11
4. Shannon 1957, pp. 4-7
5. Mahoney 1962, p. 21
6. Lizitsky 1956, pp. 206-207
7. Sharp 1952, pp. 69-81
8. Mahoney 1962, pp. 11-15
9. Goldschmidt 1959, p. 68
10. Holmberg 1952, pp. 113-123
11. Erasmus 1961, pp. 88-97
12. Erasmus 1961, pp. 26-27
13. Mead 1961, p. 65
14. Wagley 1951, p. 7
15. Devereux 1956, pp. 34-36
16. Cassel 1955, pp. 18-19
17. Sharp 1952, pp. 69-81
18. Cassel 1955, p. 37
19. Mead 1961, pp. 26-27
20. Mead 1961, pp. 60-64
21. Linton 1936, pp. 326-327
22. Mayer 1958, pp. 256-259
23. Dobyns 1957, pp. 434-444
24. Erasmus 1961, p. 105
25. Mayer 1958, p. 100
26. Erasmus 1961, p. 105
27. Foster 1962, pp. 82-83
28. Apodaca 1952, pp. 35-39
29. Foster 1957, pp. 373-375
30. Carstairs 1955, pp. 126-129
31. Carstairs 1955, p. 133
32. Barnett 1956, pp. 137-140
33. Holmberg 1960, pp. 85-87
34. Mayer 1958, pp. 260-262
35. Spicer 1952, pp. 185-193
36. Erasmus 1961, pp. 81-82
37. Mayer 1958, p. 113
38. Dobyns 1952, pp. 209-223
39. Holmberg 1960
40. Mayer 1958
41. Gillin 1960, pp. 53-54
42. Mayer 1958, pp. 188-193
43. Schweitzer 1931, pp, 110-117
44. Foster 1962, pp. 203-304
    (Communication from Dr. H. Renteln)
45. Useem 1952, pp. 261-266
46. Kimball 1955, pp. 269-293
47. Erasmus 1961, pp. 151-152
48. Erasmus 1961, pp. 79-80
49. Friedl 1959, pp. 31-35
50. Wellin 1955, pp. 73-92
51. Gould 1957, pp. 511-513
52. Adams 1957, pp. 225-231
53. Foster 1962, p. 88
54. Adams 1957, pp. 225-232
55. Holmberg 1952, pp. 122-123
56. Mayer 1958, pp. 257-258
57. Mayer 1958, pp. 207-210
58. Mead 1961, p. 89
59. Dube 1958, pp. 122-123
60. du Sautoy 1958, p. 89
61. Dube 1958, p. 71
62. Foster 1962, pp. 180-181
63. Simmons 1955, pp. 326-347
64. du Sautoy 1958, pp. 87-90
65. Mayer 1958, p. 256
66. Dube 1958, pp. 126-128
67. Holmberg 1960, pp. 82-95
68. Foster 1962, pp. 40-41
69. Hunt 1955, p. 318
70. Smith 1955, p. 361
71. Davis 1955, pp. 69-70
72. Dube 1958, pp. 120-122
73. Foster 1962, pp. 52-53
74. Mead 1956, p. 31

75. Mead 1956, pp. 141-151
76. Mead 1956, p. 241
77. Erasmus 1961, p. 241
78. Erasmus 1961, pp. 252-253
79. Du Bois 1955, p. 1233
80. Adams 1951
81. Coon 1951
82. Lewis 1960, p. 297
83. Du Bois 1955, pp. 1233-1234
84. Erasmus 1961, pp. 240-242
85. Foster 1962, pp. 187-188
    (Communication from Dr.
    Kalervo Oberg)

BIBLIOGRAPHY

1. ADAMS, JOHN B., "Culture and Conflict in an Egyptian Village," in *American Anthropologist*, Vol. 59, No. 2: 1957.
2. ADAMS, RICHARD N., "A Study of Labor Preference in Peru," in *Human Organization*, Vol. 10, No. 3: 1951.
3. APODACA, ANACLETO, "Corn and Custom," in *Human Problems in Technological Change*, ed. Edward W. Spicer, Russell Sage Foundation, New York: 1952.
4. BARNETT, HOMER G., *Anthropology in Administration*, Row, Peterson and Co., Evanston: 1956.
5. CARSTAIRS, G. MORRIS, "Medicine and Faith in Rural Rajasthan," in *Health, Culture and Community*, ed. Benjamin D. Paul, Russell Sage Foundation, New York: 1955.
6. CASSEL, JOHN, "A South African Health Program," in *Health, Culture and Community*, ed. Benjamin D. Paul, Russell Sage Foundation, New York: 1955.
7. COON, CARLETON, *Caravan: The Story of the Middle East*, Henry Holt, New York: 1951.
8. DAVIS, KINGSLEY, "Population and Change in Backward Areas," in *Underdeveloped Areas*, ed. Lyle W. Shannon, Harper and Bros., New York: 1957.
9. DEVEREUX, GEORGE, "Normal and Abnormal," in *Some Uses of Anthropology: Theoretical and Applied*, Anthropological Society of Washington, Washington, D.C.: 1956.
10. DOBYNS, HENRY F., "Experiment in Conservation," in *Human Problems in Technological Change*, ed. Edward H. Spicer, Russell Sage Foundation, New York: 1952.
11. DOBYNS, HENRY F., "Blunders with Bolsas," in *Underdeveloped Areas*, ed. Lyle W. Shannon, Harper and Bros., New York: 1957.
12. DUBE, S.C., *India's Changing Villages*, Routledge and Kegan Paul, Ltd., London: 1958.
13. DU BOIS, CORA, "The Dominant Value Profile in American Culture," in *American Anthropologist*, Vol. 57, No. 6, Pt. 1: 1955.
14. DU SAUTOY, PETER, *Community Development in Ghana*, Oxford University Press, London: 1958.
15. ERASMUS, CHARLES J., *Man Takes Control*, University of Minnesota Press, Minneapolis: 1961.

16. FOSTER, GEORGE M., "Some Social Factors Related to the Success of a Public Health Program," in *Underdeveloped Areas,* ed. Lyle W. Shannon, Harper and Bros., New York: 1957.

17. FOSTER, GEORGE M., *Traditional Cultures and the Impact of Technological Change,* Harper and Bros., New York: 1962.

18. FRASER, T.M., "Sociocultural Parameters in Directed Change," in *Human Organization,* Spring (pp. 96-98): 1963.

19. FREIDL, ERNESTINE, "The Role of Kinship in the Transmission of National Culture of Rural Villages in Mainland Greece," in *American Anthropologist,* Vol. 61, No. 1: 1959.

20. GILLIN, JOHN P., "Some Signposts for Policy," in *Social Change in Latin America Today,* Harper and Bros., New York: 1960.

21. GOLDSCHMIDT, WALTER, *Man's Way,* World Publishing Co., Cleveland: 1959.

22. GOULD HAROLD A., "The Implications of Technological Change for Folk and Scientific Medicine," in *American Anthropologist,* Vol. 59, No. 3: 1957.

23. HOLMBERG, ALLEN R., "The Wells That Failed," in *Human Problems in Technological Change,* ed. Edward H. Spicer, Russell Sage Foundation, New York: 1952.

24. HOLMBERG, ALLEN R., "Changing Community Attitudes and Values in Peru: A Case Study in Guided Change," in *Social Change in Latin America Today,* Harper and Bros., New York: 1960.

25. HUNT, CHESTER, L., "Cultural Barriers to Point Four," in *Underdeveloped Areas,* ed. Lyle W. Shannon, Harper and Bros., New York: 1957.

26. KIMBALL, SOLON, "An Alabama Town Health Survey," in *Health, Culture and Community,* ed. Benjamin D. Paul, Russell Sage Foundation, New York: 1955.

27. LEWIS, OSCAR, "Mexico Since Cardenas," in *Social Change in Latin America Today,* Harper and Bros., New York: 1960.

28. LINTON, RALPH, *The Study of Man,* Appleton-Century Co., New York: 1936.

29. LIZITSKY, GENE, *Four Ways of Being Human,* Viking Press, New York: 1956.

30. MAHONY, FRANK, *Problems of Community Development in Somalia: The Pastoral Nomads,* USOM Somalia (Mimeo): 1962.

31. MAYER, ALBERT, *Pilot Project, India,* University of California Press, Berkeley and Los Angeles: 1958.

32. MEAD, MARGARET, *New Lives for Old,* Wm. Morrow and Co., New York: 1956.

33. MEAD, MARGARET, *Cultural Patterns and Technical Change,* Mentor Books, New York: 1961.

34. SCHWEITZER, ALBERT, *The Forest Hospital at Nambarene,* Henry Holt, New York: 1931.

35. SHANNON, LYLE W., "Introduction," in *Underdeveloped Areas,* Harper and Bros., New York: 1957.

36. SHARP, LAURISTON, "Steel Axes for Stone Age Australians," in *Hu-*

man Problems in Technological Change, ed. Edward H. Spicer, Russell Sage Foundation, New York: 1952.

37. SIMMONS, OZZIE G., "The Clinical Team in a Chilean Health Center," in *Health, Culture and Community,* ed. Benjamin D. Paul, Russell Sage Foundation, New York: 1955.

38. SMITH, BRUCE L., "Communications Research on Non-Industrial Countries," in *Underdeveloped Areas,* ed. Lyle W. Shannon, Harper and Bros., New York: 1957.

39. SPICER, E. H., "Sheepmen and Technicians," in *Human Problems in Technological Change,* ed. E. H. Spicer, Russell Sage Foundation, New York: 1952.

40. USEEM, JOHN, "Democracy in Progress," in *Human Problems in Technological Change,* ed. Edward H. Spicer, Russell Sage Foundation, New York: 1952.

41. WAGLEY, CHARLES, *Cultural Hints for U.S. Personnel Going to Latin America,* Foreign Service Institute, Department of State, Washington, D.C.: 1952.

42. WELLIN, EDWARD, "Water Boiling in a Peruvian Town," in *Health, Culture and Community,* ed. Benjamin D. Paul, Russell Sage Foundation, New York: 1955.

INDEX

225